For Our Tomorrow,
They Give Their Today"

CHARLES R. "BUTCH" FARABEE JR.

National Park
RANGER
AN AMERICAN ICON

JUL 2003

DEMCO

DEDICATED TO
RANGERS OF THE "OLD SCHOOL"
Howard Chapman
Dave Karraker
Frank Kowski
Tom Thomas

AND

My Two Sons

Published by Roberts Rinehart Publishers
A Member of The Rowman & Littlefield Publishing Group, Inc.
4501 Forbes Boulevard, Suite 200
Lanham, MD 20706

Distributed by National Book Network

Library of Congress Cataloging-in-Publication Data
Farabee, Charles R.
    National park ranger : an American icon / Charles R. Farabee Jr.
    p. cm.
    Includes bibliographical references
    ISBN 1-57098-392-5 (pbk. : alk. paper)
    1. Park rangers—United States—History. 2. United States. National Park Service—
History. I. Title.
SB482.A4F37 2003
363.6'8'092—dc21

                                                        2003001022

∞™The paper used in this publication meets the minimum requirements of American National Standard for Information Sciences—Permanence of Paper for Printed Library Materials, ANSI/NISO Z39.48-1992.

Manufactured in the United States of America.

CONTENTS

The Mission of the
National Park Service

. . . To promote and regulate the use of the . . . national parks . . . which purpose is to conserve the scenery and the natural and historic objects and the wild life therein and to provide for the enjoyment of the same in such manner and by such means as will leave them unimpaired for the enjoyment of future generations.

—1916 NATIONAL PARK SERVICE ORGANIC ACT, 16 U.S.C. 1

FOREWORD

I am proud to be the sixteenth Director of the National Park Service, and to be able to wear the uniform of "green and gray." I appreciate the heritage it stands for and the rich traditions to be maintained. Perhaps second only to liberty, our national parks are our nation's finest legacy to future generations.

I began my career in park management over thirty years ago, having recently served as the Director of the Division of Recreation and Parks for the State of Florida. I know that the strength of our parks—whether local, state, or national—lies in the people who protect and serve them: these men and women are truly special. They are devoted to the past, vigilant in the present, and optimistic for the future. Our employees, regardless in what capacity they may work— maintenance, administration, research, concessions, law enforcement, resources management, in partnerships and with volunteers, planning, visitor services and interpretation—are fortunate to be able to build on the foundation of dedication and talent of those who came before.

The ideals of preservation, good stewardship, and serving visitors to our national parks are my beacons, guiding the National Park Service in caring for these special places promised to the future, the places where our nation's heritage and hopes are preserved. I am glad to say that the National Park Service is now beginning to reflect our nation's rich diversity and ethnicity, and that its employees are coming to their tasks armed with a greater sophistication than ever before.

With a National Park Service career spanning four decades, Butch Farabee brings considerable field experience to writing this book on park rangers. Proudly wearing the "flat hat" in nine park areas across the country, he served in a variety of positions from field ranger to park superintendent and has received numerous honors, including the Service's Harry Yount Lifetime Achievement Award, conferred by me in 2001. Butch was the first President of the Association of National Park Rangers. He has exemplified the professionalism and skill of a ranger and this book reflects his dedication and loyalty to his life's work.

Serving as Director of the National Park Service is an honor and a privilege, and I am pleased to stand with the rangers, the men and women of the National Park Service, every day, as they protect and care for the national parks. I hope that this book brings you closer to the work of our rangers, and as always, I'll see you in the parks!

Fran P. Mainella
Director
National Park Service

Fran P. Mainella, Director, National Park Service

INTRODUCTION
THE NATIONAL PARK RANGER

If a trail is to be blazed, send a ranger, if an animal is floundering in the snow, send a ranger, if a bear is in a hotel, send a ranger, if a fire threatens a forest, send a ranger, and if someone needs to be saved, send a ranger.

—STEPHEN T. MATHER,
FIRST DIRECTOR OF THE NATIONAL PARK SERVICE

National Park Rangers are an amalgam of Jedi Knight, favorite teacher, and Smokey Bear. As stewards of our nation's treasures, they are heir to five thousand years of tradition: they celebrate this legacy with pride, reflect it with humility. It is a privilege to be called ranger; but the title must be *earned*, gained through credibility, confidence, and ardor. Their reputation is hard won, they profit from those laboring before them: a rough mix of explorer, pioneer, conservationist, lawman, and teacher. Job description alone does not make a rangers, and they certainly are not rangers just because a visitor says so. It is attitude and choice; a fervor for the resource and dedication to public service.

Some rangers do it all: protection, interpretation, and resource management as policeman, educator, fireman, manager, interpreter, rescuer, and all-around caretaker of our country's heritage. Others dedicate an entire career to one discipline like emergency response, environmental education, endangered animals, wilderness protection, or history. In some parks these men and women actually have broader responsibilities than almost anyone else within government. And, only with the exception of our country's elite military units, no group has as much talent, commitment, and passion as do those who proudly wear the "green and gray." They are a sentimental link between the "old West" and the "new." Meet three National Park Rangers who exemplify the finest of their profession as well as embodying the mission of the National Park Service.

Larry Van Slyke recently finished his thirty-two-year Park Service career as Chief Ranger of Utah's Canyonlands National Park. He was an inspiration for young and old alike. Even before graduating from high school he knew he wanted to wear the "flat hat" like the men he so admired in nearby Rocky Mountain National Park. Athletic and an accomplished outdoorsman, he began his long service career eradicating diseased trees, fighting forest fires, and maintaining hiking trails while attending college.

Larry served as a field ranger from Florida to Alaska, seeing duty in the Everglades, Colorado's Black Canyon of the Gunnison, Rocky Mountain, Grand Canyon, Alaska's remote Lake Clark National Park, Zion, and Canyonlands. While serving as Climbing Ranger on Rocky Mountain's 14,255-foot-high Longs Peak he clawed his way up the 1,500-foot face of "The Diamond," a dangerously demanding rock climb. Over the years his skill and courage have literally saved dozens of lives while participating in hundreds of daring rescues, including Colorado's devastating Big Thompson Canyon Flood in 1976 in which 134 people died. Van Slyke deserves the numerous awards earned for his many contributions and heroics, including the Department of Interior's Valor Award.

Larry is a veteran ranger-pilot with nearly 2,000 hours of flying the Service's small float planes into "bush" Alaska, checking on hunters, watching for illegal mining, searching for lost aircraft, and just keeping an eye on the wilderness he loves. On duty at the Grand Canyon, he was responsible for the innermost secrets of the mile-deep park, patrolling the Colorado River and refining his white-water and rafting skills. A trained law enforcement officer for thirty years and a graduate of the FBI Academy, he has issued citations, made arrests for major crimes, and participated in statewide manhunts for killers. As both a "grunt" and then supervisory firefighter, he was often dispatched around the country to battle wildland fires. As an emergency medic for twenty years, he used his advanced training to care for hundreds of the sick and injured.

Ranger Deb Liggett oversees nearly nine million acres of wild Alaska and as the superintendent of four separate park areas, she does a superb job. In her heart, however, she is a National Park Service interpreter. She has long been an inspiration to those others who have also dedicated their lives to enriching our understanding of the world around us. As a seasonal ranger at Colorado's Great Sand Dunes National Monument and for the next fifteen years of her career, Deb promoted education and wonder through provocation and revelation. As a field interpreter, she has worked from coast to coast in seven demanding and diverse park areas. Armed with a wealth of knowledge, she is quick to captivate an audience with her charisma and pointed homespun humor. Great interpreters—like Deb—have a passion for the subject and a love of people.

While standing on the edge of the Grand Canyon, Ranger Liggett has subtly led park visitors back two billion years, to when the earth was young and raw. She has helped a Civil War buff gain knowledge of Dr. Samuel Mudd, imprisoned off the coast of Florida after unwittingly aiding President Abraham Lincoln's assassin. Deb has eased the fears of more than one camper in Big Bend by patiently explaining that the howls heard just before sunrise were not really wolves, but a few talkative coyotes.

Deb Liggett watched Hurricane Andrew literally rip "her" Visitor Center apart while helping lead the team that closed down Everglades National Park as the monster storm approached. Four years later she was back, this time giving a heartfelt speech when the new facility was dedicated; proudly, she put up the flag one more time.

Interpreters are the heart and soul of the National Park Service. They inspire visitors to seek out and understand the mysteries couched in wonder and beauty before them. This is done through talks, walks, demonstrations, pictures, living history, story-telling, and in a hundred other exciting ways. A master of many trades, Deb has coordinated publications, edited brochures, designed exhibits, and been involved with interpretive planning. And, like many rangers, she has helped VIPs like presidents, Cabinet secretaries, and foreign dignitaries enjoy our parks. As a role model, educator, and "Interpreter's Interpreter," Ranger Deb Liggett proudly does all of this and more.

Jack Potter, unlike Van Slyke or Liggett, both of whom moved from park to park, has dedicated his more than three-decade career to a single area much larger than the state of Rhode Island. Jack is the Assistant Chief Ranger of Glacier National Park and is responsible for a wide variety of critical management and resource issues within this northern Montana wilderness of one million acres. Potter, for his devotion to and understanding of this world-renowned natural and cultural resource, is recognized professionally by his peers as a "Ranger's Ranger," richly deserving of the awards and numerous testimonials he routinely receives.

Potter manages the park programs dealing with its plants and animals, including the welfare of the grizzly bear, gray wolf, and bald eagle, all of which are endangered species. He then strives to physically eradicate those species that are exotic, or nonnative. Jack helps monitor the quality of the region's air and water and oversees several programs that address critical issues such as these. He supervises a plant nursery used in replanting park areas needing rehabilitation. He commonly deals with illegal horse and cattle trespass, as well as the theft of timber by the park's neighbors. In addition to both these and other resource management duties, he oversees the upkeep of nearly eight hundred miles of hiking and horse trails used by many of the park's two million visitors.

A Grand Canyon ranger points the way in this 1910 advertisement for the Santa Fe's California Limited.
NATIONAL PARK SERVICE, HARPERS FERRY CENTER ARCHIVES

Potter, an accomplished outdoorsman, is both an avid mountaineer and hiker, as well as a highly- proficient river runner and skier. He is an expert horseman and can pack a mule with the best. This veteran ranger uses these skills to assess the "health" of the fragile resources in his care. Every year he travels many hundreds of miles of trails to evaluate them for needed repairs while providing supervision to the crews that maintain them.

There is hardly a park peak Jack hasn't climbed, most more than once. While scrambling upwards and without seeming to breath hard, he can recite the scientific and common names of the plants you pass, as well as provide a running commentary on the ecology in which they exist. Ranger

Potter is an encyclopedia on the region's human history and can articulate the often contentious and always convoluted politics for an area that shares its border with Canada, the Blackfeet Indian Nation, the Forest Service, and some local landowners who still believe neither the park nor the federal government should exist.

Like life itself, a ranger's day often seems to have more than its share of the ordinary and mundane: Screen applicants for a job. Attend meetings. Dig pit toilets. Build partnerships. Budget for the coming season. Pick up trash. Administer. Build. Clean. Coordinate. Critique. Fire. Hire. Inspect. Meet. Network. Patrol. Plan. Study. Supervise. Talk. Train. Write. Rangers perform hundreds of common chores to maintain the park while helping people to enjoy it. Even in the routine, however, rangers are heroes. Not by saving a life, teaching a kid, or protecting a bear, but by guarding and perpetuating this country's irreplaceable natural and cultural treasures for generations yet unborn. They do it with skill, insight, and genuine passion, and . . . make it seem easy.

> ## The Successful Ranger
>
> . . . must be honest, courteous, and patient and at the same time firm, equal to emergencies, and of good judgment. He must be impartial to all, cognizant of his responsibilities, and loyal to the Service he represents. To find men in whom all of these qualifications are happily combined is not easy, but when once found they should be encouraged in every possible way, for when all is said and done it is the ranger, the man who deals more directly with the public than any other, that reflects the attitude of the Service he represents.
>
> —YOSEMITE
> SUPERINTENDENT'S
> ANNUAL REPORT TO THE DIRECTOR, 1918

Most rangers believe they have the best job in the world. Death Valley ranger Dennis Burnett agrees. PHOTO COURTESY DENNIS BURNETT

Chapter 1
THE RANGER
GENESIS OF AN IDEA

The concept of the ranger as a "guardian of the land" goes back five thousand years to Mesopotamian drawings on temple and palace walls. Desert "rangers" patrolled the southern frontier of what is now Egypt, a thousand years later. Between 1100 and 200 B.C., "preserve men" in ancient China, Persia, and later in Greece and Rome protected forests, hunting grounds, parks, and sacred groves from the commoners.

Royal forests appeared in medieval Europe as early as A.D. 500 and foresters served German, Norman, and English aristocrats for the next nine hundred years. The English word "ranger" evolved from the Germanic "ring" or "range" in the early 1300s and then appeared as a title in the English Royal Rolls of the mid-fourteenth century. As trusted officers of the realm, they were appointed to safeguard imperial forests from trespass and woodcutting and to prevent the wild game of the nobility from being poached.

Roving militia guarded the frontiers of the American New World from Indian attack as early as 1629. By 1682, "rangers" in Colonial Virginia were assigned by the House of Burgesses to protect vulnerable settlements along the major rivers. In Colonial South Carolina and Florida, ranger battalions were used in military forays against the Spanish in the 1720s. Elite fighting units like Rogers' Rangers served with distinction in the British Army during the French and Indian Wars. Twenty years later, American ranger units were used against England during the American Revolution. With nearly 350 years of sacrifice and honor, rangers herald a proud tradition in this nation's military to this day.

Following the Revolutionary War, the best known American frontier ranger group was the Texas Rangers. Loosely organized in 1823 by Stephen

Austin to fight hostiles while Texans pushed westward, they were authorized by the state in 1835; the celebrated law enforcement branch was formally created in 1874. With missions similar to those trusted officers in Texas, rangers could also be found in Arizona, New Mexico, and California.

The Forest Reserve Act of 1891 created large parcels out of federal western public domain (later called national forests), and seven years later forest rangers were finally assigned to protect these isolated, wooded mountainous tracts. Forest rangers for the national parks appeared almost simultaneously in 1898 when civilians began to assist the United States Army in guarding Yosemite, Sequoia, and General Grant National Parks.

The earliest known use of the term "park ranger" occurred in1901 in the Sequoia National Park Superintendent's annual report. In succeeding years it became increasingly more common to call the forest rangers in national parks "park rangers." In a 1904 letter to the Secretary of the Interior, the Acting Superintendent of Sequoia requested that an individual on his staff be appointed as a "Deputy Park Ranger." Finally, the title "Park Ranger" became official in the national parks in California in 1905. "Forest rangers" in these three areas were designated "park rangers" on creation of the United States Forest Service and the resulting simultaneous transfer of these forest reserves out of the Department of the Interior to the new agency's current home, the Department of Agriculture.

THE FIRST PARK RANGERS

A Ranger's Duty Is to Protect . . .

. . . the park from the people,

the people from the park, and

the people from the people.

As early as 1696, there were caretakers of a park-like area in Maryland, and in 1859 men on horseback patrolled New York City's Central Park. It wasn't until the federal government dedicated California's remote Yosemite Valley to the future, however, that the era of the "modern" park ranger began.

Galen Clark: Guardian of Yosemite

On June 30, 1864, a war-weary President Lincoln signed the Yosemite Grant Act into law. The United States now had the first "jewel in its crown" of special places. Yosemite Valley and the nearby Mariposa Grove of Big Trees were placed into the public trust; those sixty square miles granted to the State of California through federal legislation and made a state park at the time were to be the genesis of the national park idea. This was the first area set aside anywhere in the world by the government of a country purely for its scenic value. On May 21, 1866, Yosemite pioneer Galen Clark was named "Guardian of Yosemite" by a nine-member State Commission (of which he was one) and was duly authorized to protect these won-drous areas. Guardian Clark's wages were "not to exceed five hundred dollars per annum," as the first protection officer in this new type of park.

First seeing the splendors of Yosemite in 1855, only four years after Europeans first entered the area, Galen Clark received his appointment at age fifty-two. A widower, he left his five children with relatives when he first moved to California in 1853. Packer, miner, rancher, road builder, and guide, he was the first non-Indian to see the remote corners of the Mariposa Grove. In addi-tion to being an early homesteader and innkeeper, he was also a regular explorer of nearby Yosemite Valley. Clark was ideal for the job; interest, dedication, and ardor would eventually earn him the title "Mister Yosemite."

Galen Clark was the first state park ranger, beginning as "Guardian of Yosemite" in 1864, when Yosemite Valley was a state park. NATIONAL PARK SERVICE, YOSEMITE NATIONAL PARK RESEARCH LIBRARY

The appointing commissioners spelled out Guardian Clark's duties in an eight-page letter. These instructions would mirror what the men and women of the National Park Service do today. They—Clark and a subguardian he imme-diately appointed, by the name of Peter Longhurst—were to protect the area and accommodate the users, an often impossible dichotomy still vexing rangers to this day. The Valley was a "crazy quilt of roads, hotels, cabins, and pastures and pens for cattle, hogs, mules, and horses." State laws then recently enacted to protect the new park were to be strictly enforced by the duo. Trees were not to be cut, fires were to be monitored, building was to be controlled, and what little infrastructure then in existence, such as trails, bridges, and lad-ders up the cliffs, was to be maintained. They were given authority to "prevent either visitors or settlers from doing anything which would tend to impair the Valley or its surroundings." He would issue leases and business concessions to those early settlers.

Two years after Congress set Yosemite aside in 1864, the California Legislature enacted the first park-protection laws. Violations could result in a maximum fine of $500 and imprisonment for up to six months, standard penalties that still exist today. Clark and Longhurst were required to be "during the season of visitors, at least—always in or about the valley and Big Tree Grove, in order to bring about entire safety and security that wanton damages will not be inflicted." In 1870 Clark made an arrest—a first within a park—for a felled giant pine tree; found guilty, the men responsible were fined $20 each by a local judge. Clark was even made a special sheriff's deputy in 1875 to help evict a nearby and longtime associate from his home in the Valley.

While he fought fires and protected resources, Clark shared his love and knowledge of the region through education and as a guide. John Muir—a legend in early conservation—was greatly influenced by Clark, whom he called, "the best mountaineer I ever met, and one of the most sincere tree-lovers I ever knew." Finally, with twenty-two years of loyal and dedicated service on two separate tours (1866–1880 and 1889–1897), he retired in 1897, at age eighty-three. On March 24, 1910, Galen Clark died in his sleep in Oakland, California, and now rests in the cemetery in his beloved Yosemite.

Harry S. Yount and the Yellowstone Custodians

In April 1873, the year after Yellowstone National Park was created, Nathaniel P. Langford, the park's first superintendent, appointed David E. Folsom to look after the park. The following year, Langford designated hotel keeper James Mc-Cartney (along with several dozen other people) as "custodian" for the summer. In 1875, U. S. Deputy Marshall John H. "Yellowstone Jack" Baronett from Bozeman chased horse thieves across Yellowstone in the first recorded law enforcement incident involving a national park. Baronett was not officially affiliated with the park at that time.

On April 19, 1877, three years after his initial appointment, McCartney received specific written instructions from Yellowstone's second Superintendent, Philetus W. Norris, to protect the park. He was to "guard well and enjoin others to do so, against wanton slaughter of game, spoliation of Geyser cones and other curiosities, and especially against forest fires." Working without pay, McCartney took care of the area until Norris arrived in late summer. That same year, Chief Joseph led a small band of Nez Perce through the park for two weeks; actively pursued by the Army, they headed north for the Canadian border. McCartney was forced to get involved when a park visitor was killed in his hotel's front door, and he buried another (in a wooden bath tub) who died in the skirmish. He then helped several more terrified visitors make their way back to safety at Mammoth.

"Rocky Mountain" Harry Yount, the first National Park ranger, circa 1873.
NATIONAL PARK SERVICE, HARPERS FERRY CENTER ARCHIVES

In the first week of July 1879, a James McCawley (not to be confused with James McCartney) earned the ignominy of being the first person arrested in a national park: drunk and disorderly. Having also lost a fistfight the night before, he tried the next day to ambush some of the men he thought responsible for the assault. Superintendent Norris sent N. D. Johnson—possessing some legal experience as a former Probate Judge in Montana but now working for the park on road construction—to make the arrest. Jailed overnight, McCawley was taken in front of a judge in Bozeman. Since the crime had actually taken place in the Wyoming Territory and not Montana, the authorities refused to accept the prisoner, and the case was quickly dismissed for lack of legal jurisdiction.

Harry S. Yount—christened Henry and probably born in 1839—was hired as gamekeeper for Yellowstone on June 21, 1880, earning $1,000 a year, a significant sum since the park's annual budget was just $15,000. Yount, typical of many men roaming the West, had been dispossessed following the Civil War, after serving twice for the Union. Mustered out as Company Quartermaster Sergeant, he drifted to the Wyoming Territory, working as a bullwhacker and then as a guide and packer for the Hayden Geological Survey for seven summers. Hunting had been legal since the park's creation, but serious abuses occurred and caused major concern. Commercial hunters slaughtered the elk for their hides, and other practices drastically affected wildlife populations. The park's answer was to preserve at least token herds of these animals in the northeast section of the park. It was the job of "Rocky Mountain Harry" to protect these animals from market hunters. He was to report on the wildlife, and utilizing his skills earned as a professional hunter, also to provide meat for park personnel. After fourteen months he resigned in September 1881, complaining that the park was too large to patrol:

Yellowstone tourist Charles Kenck became the first recorded death in a national park when he was killed by Nez Perce Indians fleeing the U.S. Army, on August 26, 1877.

> I do not think that any one man appointed by the honorable Secretary, and specifically designated as a game-keeper, is what is needed . . . but a small and reliable police force of men, employed when needed . . . is what is really the most practicable way of seeing that the game is protected from wanton slaughter, the forests from careless use of fire, and the enforcement of all the other laws, rules and regulations for the protection and improvement of the park.

Officials soon abandoned the position of gamekeeper. Yount died in Wheatland, Wyoming, on May 16, 1924, but was still credited as the first "national park ranger." In reality, James McCartney should at least share in this recognition.

Congress gave Yellowstone $40,000 in 1883 to pay the superintendent as well as to employ ten assistants, at least nine of whom were actually hired by the Secretary of the Interior at $900 each. Congress intended for them to be a police force and protect the park from poachers and vandalism. They were to fight fires, guard the wildland and geyser formations, and provide information. Superintendent Conger, however, viewed them merely as guides. In retrospect, it appears both they and Conger were ineffective.

In 1884 the Wyoming Territorial Legislature extended the law to Yellowstone, and a justice of the peace and constables were placed in the park. These men, along with the assistant superintendents, arrested violators and brought them before the justice of the peace. Fines were levied and the money split between the judge and the arresting officials. Abuse of this system, described by some observers as "notoriously inefficient if not positively corrupt" and scorn of the constables as "rabbit catchers" by the Montana newspapers, finally caused their authority to be repealed on March 19, 1886. The management and protection rendered by the civilian administration of Yellowstone was an almost total failure. Congress cut off funds and the superintendent and his assistants were no longer needed. In dire need of competent managers, the Secretary of the Interior turned to the United States Army for assistance.

$1,000 REWARD!

MR. L. R. PIPER, Cashier of the First National Bank of St. Marys, Ohio, arrived at the Fountain Hotel, in the Yellowstone National Park, as a tourist, on the 29th day of July, 1900, and disappeared from the hotel on the evening of the 30th, and has not been seen or heard from since that time.

DESCRIPTION:

Age, 36; Height, 5 feet 9 inches; Weight, 130 pounds; Complexion, sandy; Color of Hair, light, inclined to reddish tinge; Nose, slightly crooked; smooth-shaven face. Wore blue suit with dark check about one inch wide; no vest; soft-bosomed white shirt, with initials "L. R. P." at bottom of bosom, embroidered in red. Black patent leather lace shoes, laces much broken. Two diamond rings, one Knight Templar emblem, a Shriner's button in lapel of coat. Dark Derby hat.

The First National Bank of St. Marys, O., wires me as follows:

"**MRS. L. R. PIPER** offers a reward of **ONE THOUSAND DOLLARS** for the finding of Piper, or his body, if dead.

"Signed,   FIRST NATIONAL BANK."

Aug. 10, 1900.   Address,

J. H. DEAN,
Supt. Y. P. A., M. H. Springs, Wyoming.

Despite a sizable reward for its time, as well as a month-long search by the Army, the fate of 36-year-old LeRoy Piper is still unknown. NATIONAL PARK SERVICE, YELLOWSTONE NATIONAL PARK

Chapter 2
THE SOLDIERS

The United States Army played a pivotal role in the early protection and administration of the first four national parks: Yellowstone, Sequoia, General Grant, and Yosemite. This country owes these men a great deal of gratitude for helping to preserve these areas for future generations.

YELLOWSTONE NATIONAL PARK

For more than a decade after Congress established Yellowstone, the park was under serious threat from those who would exploit its resources. Vandals and souvenir seekers chipped away at geyser cones and mineral springs. Animals were slaughtered. Developers erected ramshackle camps for tourists without always having permission. Five civilian superintendents were hired to guard this land from 1872 to 1886, but they lacked experience, funds, and manpower. These men were unable to protect the vast park, and in 1886 Congress finally refused to appropriate any further money for such ineffectiveness and incompetence. Since no one was willing to serve without pay, Yellowstone now lacked any semblance of protection. Invoking the Sundry Civil Act of 1883, the Secretary of the Interior called upon the Secretary of War for assistance.

On August 17, 1886, Troop M, First United States Cavalry, Fort Custer, Montana Territory, under the command of Medal of Honor recipient Captain Moses Harris, rode into the park. With him were two lieutenants, twenty enlisted men, fifty-six horses, seventeen mules, three army wagons, and one ambulance. Erecting six temporary stations throughout the park, the soldiers

The United States Army guarded several parks from 1886 to 1914. This 1911 photo shows soldiers at Yellowstone National Park headquarters at Mammoth.
NATIONAL PARK SERVICE, YELLOWSTONE NATIONAL PARK ARCHIVES

were initially based in interim frame buildings at the foot of the Mammoth Hot Spring Terraces. After the men endured five harsh winters in what was called Camp Sheridan, Congress provided $50,000 for a more permanent post at what is now park headquarters. Renamed Fort Yellowstone, the first structure was finished in 1891, and the final one, a chapel of native sandstone, in 1913. Nine different Army units served the park over the next three decades—the First, Third, Fourth, Fifth, Sixth, Seventh, Eighth, Eleventh, and Thirteenth Cavalries. At the height of the Army's presence, there were 324 soldiers, plus some families and civilian employees. They were quartered in fifteen stations and nineteen snowshoe cabins in many of the isolated corners of the park.

Paid $13 per month, plus food and clothes, troopers occupied themselves fighting fires, protecting natural features, assisting visitors, building roads and related infrastructure, and patrolling the vast backcountry for poachers. During the military's occupation of Yellowstone, hundreds of miles of roads were surveyed and then constructed by the Corps of Engineers, including the still-used "loop" road. Largely orchestrated by Captain Hiram Chittenden, these roads, he believed, should be kept "as nearly as possible in their natural condition, unchanged by the hand of man."

Regulations were written and posted conspicuously, with detachments guarding the major attractions. Until 1914, no law had real force to protect the park, but the Army evicted trouble makers and forbade their return anyway. Their first success came in early 1887 at Norris Junction when a patrol discovered William James, a local teamster, trapping beaver in the meadows along the Gibbon River. Captain Harris gladly expelled James from the park. One of the park's most important events took place in 1894, when soldiers on patrol arrested Ed Howell for slaughtering bison. Emerson Hough, a prominent journalist, happened to be present and generated national interest in the problem. Within two months Congress responded to the pressure, and the Yellowstone Protection Act (Lacey Act) became law, finally safeguarding Yellowstone and other parks subsequently.

In 1897, George Anderson, the third military superintendent of the park, wrote: "As a consequence of their good work, the beauties of the park are no longer defaced; no fires have ravaged the forests; poaching has diminished to a small percentage of what it was ten years ago, and more than all, order exists everywhere."

S. B. M. Young served as Acting Superintendent of Yosemite in 1896 and then went to Yellowstone in 1897 and 1898. After commanding a division in the Spanish-American War, in 1898 he became the Chief of Staff of the U.S. Army, serving President Theodore Roosevelt. Colonel Young was not as impressed as Captain Anderson had been with the idea of soldiers being the ultimate guardians of Yellowstone. President Roosevelt had instructed the retired Army officer to design a plan to replace the military in the park. Young recorded the following in a 1907 report:

> **The Army Is Assigned to Yellowstone: Act of March 3, 1883**
>
> "The Secretary of War, upon the request of the Secretary of the Interior, is hereby authorized and directed to make the necessary details of troops to prevent trespassers or intruders from entering the park for the purpose of destroying the game or objects of curiosity therein, or for any other purpose prohibited by law, and to remove such persons from the park if found therein."

Two years' experience in governing the park with troops and comparing the results of enforcing due observance of all rules, regulations, and instructions through the troops, and through the few (civilian) scouts that in reality are civil guides, leaves no doubt in my mind about the superiority of a trained and well-governed civil guard for this particular and difficult duty. While I found some excellent, intelligent, and conscientious noncommissioned officers and privates who have taken interest in carrying out their instructions in park duties, the majority are indifferent and appear to resent being required to subserve both the military interest and the interest of the park, on their small pay.

Young proposed a Yellowstone National Park Guard. He recommended the area be divided into four districts, with a chief inspector, four assistant inspectors, and twenty civilian guards constituting the entire protection force. During the busy period, this was to be increased with seasonal assistance. Roosevelt lost interest in the effort, however, and the Interior was unwilling to implement change, so nothing happened until 1916.

In 1916 Congress created the National Park Service, and on October 24 a civilian organization arrived to ease Yellowstone away from the Army; twenty-one soldiers (at $100 per month each) elected to remain and become park rangers. On the following June 26, however, the Army had

Troop F, Sixth United States Cavalry, on the Fallen Monarch in Yosemite in 1899.
NATIONAL PARK SERVICE, YOSEMITE NATIONAL PARK RESEARCH LIBRARY

to dismiss these very same rangers because Congress failed to provide funds for the new agency; the Army then returned to Yellowstone. For the next year, Acting Supervisor Chester A. Lindsley of the Department of the Interior and Lieutenant Colonel E. M. Leary of the Seventh Cavalry ran the park and were responsible for law enforcement and protection. Yellowstone National Park served three masters—the roads were under the Corps of Engineers, the cavalry under control of the Secretary of War, while the park's military acting superintendents reported to both the Departments of the Army and the Interior.

SEQUOIA, YOSEMITE, AND GENERAL GRANT NATIONAL PARKS

President Benjamin Harrison signed the Sequoia Act on September 25, 1890, followed six days later by the Yosemite and General Grant Act. Congress established these three areas as "public parks" or "forest reservations" (the term "national park" was never used) and placed them under the control of the Secretary of the Interior. In both Acts, Congress directed the Secretary to "provide for the preservation from injury of all timber, mineral deposits, natural curiosities or wonders . . . and their retention in their natural condition."

The successful military administration of Yellowstone prompted the same type of control in these new parks in California. In writing the two laws, Congress closely followed the wording in the Yellowstone Act. In doing so, however, it once again failed to provide either legal or financial mechanisms for the parks' protection and preservation. A month later the Secretary of the Interior noted the omission and said that "whether the parks shall be put under charge of civil custodians or a military cavalry guard shall be sent to each is a subject now being considered and investigated." The law authorizing troops in Yellowstone was not applicable to the California parks, and no legal basis existed to use the Army in Sequoia, Yosemite, or General Grant. Nevertheless, realizing these areas needed protection, the Secretary of the Interior still looked to Yellowstone for precedent and on October 21, 1890, requested that the Secretary of War detail cavalry to the new parks. This illegal use of the Army in these areas was finally addressed by Congress in 1896.

In 1891, the U.S. Cavalry began patrolling Sequoia, General Grant (four square miles of Sequoia trees later incorporated into Kings Canyon National Park), and Yosemite. The military rode into Yosemite on May 19 under the command of Captain Abram E. Wood. As in Yellowstone and Sequoia (General Grant was overseen by Sequoia) the Army's local senior officer also served as the park's acting superintendent. Since Yosemite Valley would remain under state control until 1906, the army had responsibility for everything in Yosemite National Park but the Valley and the Mariposa Grove. The soldiers blazed trails, mapped the rugged country, fought forest fires, patrolled for illegal mining, posted boundaries, and probably most important, tried to rid the park of trespassing livestock. Business was booming and within a month of the troopers' arrival that first year, they arrested four sheepherders, only to find no law authorized prosecution of the violators. Quick to improvise, they resolved the dilemma by expelling the herders on one side of the park and their flocks on the other.

From 1891 to 1914 it was customary to station men in the parks only during the summer months, hoping a hostile winter would protect the resource. Depending on the year, up to four troops (a troop consisted of approximately fifty men) were dispatched from the Presidio in San Francisco in May; half went to Yosemite and the other half to Sequoia. Their 250-mile march took two weeks, until they began using the train in 1900. That same year, soldiers were authorized to prevent trespassers from entering the three parks. In Yosemite, troops first garrisoned in Wawona, and then in 1906 "Fort Yosemite" was established in the Valley. Yosemite eventually saw both the Twenty-fourth Mounted Infantry and the Ninth Cavalry: African-American units, who were also known as "Buffalo Soldiers." Soldiers were no longer needed in General Grant, since in 1901 the four-square-mile park had been totally fenced and then placed under a civilian guard.

In 1914 the soldiers left for good, replaced by a small cadre of civilian rangers. Things had substantially changed since the military first came to the parks. In the beginning, the three California areas had been surrounded by people accustomed to unfettered use of the mountains for grazing, hunting, and woodcutting. Once park neighbors understood the issues and the limitations, the soldiers ended up assuming extralegal functions such as registering visitors and collecting tolls, checking vehicles, sealing firearms, guiding tourists and searching for those lost, reading stream gauges, fighting fires, reporting on game seen, and planting fish. Though it was often outside the traditional military experience, most soldiers found the duty both desirable and interesting.

Conservationist John Muir would eventually say of the military in the parks, "Blessings on Uncle Sam's soldiers. They have done the job well, and every pine tree is waving its arms for joy."

These Sequoia rangers—Lew Davis, Ernest Britten, Charlie Blossom, and Harry Britten—are each wearing two badges, circa 1902. The upper one is the Department of Interior badge, but no one is quite certain what the bottom one is.
NATIONAL PARK SERVICE, SEQUOIA NATIONAL PARK ARCHIVES

Chapter 3
EARLY RANGERS

YOSEMITE NATIONAL PARK

Not only was the Army "guarding" Yellowstone, it also drew duty in California's three national parks, each signed into law by President Benjamin Harrison in 1890. When the Spanish-American War broke out on April 25, 1898, and the Army left for Cuba, the General Land Office—as they did for Sequoia—recommended local civilians be hired to patrol and provide some sort of official presence. Eleven men were sworn in on June 24 as "forest agents" for Yosemite. They provided their own riding stock, weapons, and supplies and received either $3 or $4 a day, depending on whether they were in the southern or northern end of the park. It was a short war, and the regular cavalry rode back into Yosemite in 1899, staying until 1914.

Before they had a chance to learn their job, however, the original eleven forest agents were dismissed. Archie C. Leonard at fifty-two and Charles T. Leidig, the first white boy to be born in Yosemite thirty-six years before, were promptly rehired for the winter for the park's nearly fifteen hundred square miles. Capable mountaineers and well prepared for the job in many respects, Leonard and Leidig were the first two to carry the title of ranger (either forest or park) in a national park, preceding Sequoia's Ernest Britten by more than a year.

The few rangers for the park were paid out of the Sierra Forest Reserve funds and were issued forest reserve ranger badges. In Sequoia's *Superintendent's Annual Report of 1901*, the park's military supervisor first used the term "park ranger" even though four more years would pass before "forest ranger" was officially changed to "park ranger."

In 1902 the Secretary of the Interior approved three categories of rangers. A Class 1 was expected to be familiar with the woods, to scale timber, to survey,

Rangers at Yosemite in 1915. NATIONAL PARK SERVICE, YOSEMITE NATIONAL PARK RESEARCH LIBRARY

The first auto to enter a national park was on June 23, 1900, in Yosemite. On January 6, 1902, the same man drove another vehicle to the rim of the Grand Canyon, also a first. On July 24, 1908, $5 was charged for a car in Mt. Rainier National Park, the first such fee. On September 3, 1915, one person was killed when a car rolled off the road in Yellowstone National Park, probably the Service's first fatal motor vehicle accident.

and "to direct and report intelligently on the ordinary work of the reserve." Classes 2 and 3 had no special requirements, "but they must be able-bodied, sober, and industrious men, fully capable of comprehending and following their instructions." Class 1 earned $90 per month, Class 2 earned $75, and Class 3 earned $60. Britten was a Class 1 and the rest were Class 2. Leidig, Leonard, and their fellow rangers were probably constantly confused since Yosemite Valley fell under California jurisdiction, and the park's remaining 1,457 square miles came under federal rule. The two areas were not joined until June 11, 1906.

Leidig soon proved a disappointment. He flagrantly hunted within the park and routinely turned a blind eye when his friends did the same. The park's Army Commander, Acting Superintendent Harry C. Benson, frequently complained to the Secretary of the Interior about Leidig's many transgressions, rampant "cronyism," and blatant misappropriation of government property; he was finally dismissed in 1907. On the other hand, Leonard was conscientious and energetic, serving admirably as a park ranger for another ten years before finally retiring at seventy-one in 1917. He was to witness two of the park's greatest events—the arrival of the first automobile in 1900 (the first in any national park), and the passage of the Raker Act in 1913, which authorized the damming of the Tuolumne River in Hetch Hetchy to provide domestic water for San Francisco.

SEQUOIA AND GENERAL GRANT NATIONAL PARKS

As they did in Yosemite, soldiers would leave San Francisco's Presidio early each May bound for a summer in Sequoia and General Grant National Parks. Control of illegal sheep grazing (sometimes cattle) in the lush meadows of the high mountains was their primary function. Most important, however, they established a federal presence—albeit seasonal—with the settlers and ranchers of the area. When the Spanish-American War erupted, their services were temporarily needed elsewhere. Left without a visible authority in the valuable resource, the Department of the Interior turned to the nearby General Land Office. Assistant special forest agents were authorized in June 1898, to guard neighboring forest lands as well as the two parks until the Army returned. Their days would be long and the work would be hard.

Receiving his appointment that summer at age thirty-six, Ernest Britten was the first of an eventual six assistant special forest agents to work in Sequoia (and General Grant). A married man who was raised on the park's doorstep, he was friendly, honest, and outgoing. Mostly, however, he was available and needed a steady-paying job. He received $4 a day and furnished all his own supplies, including horses and saddles. In the early years he lived outside the park and patrolled the backcountry, fought forest fires, and tried to eject the "hoofed locust," as sheep were less-than-fondly labeled. That first summer Britten answered to the Sierra Forest Reserve (predecessor of the Forest Service) and shared duties between the nearby forest and the two parks. Two thousand sheep were removed from Sequoia that year, and considerable fire fighting tested his endurance due to a prolonged drought.

Photographed circa 1915 with his wife, Ernest Britten was ranger-in-charge at Sequoia National Park from 1900 to 1905, when he elected to transfer to the Forest Service.
NATIONAL PARK SERVICE, HARPERS FERRY CENTER ARCHIVES

The rangers of 1938 were like their professional descendants: dedicated and skilled.
NATIONAL PARK SERVICE, ROCKY MOUNTAIN NATIONAL PARK ARCHIVES

Other Early "Rangers"

Area	Year Created	Name	On Duty
Casa Grande (AZ)	1889	Frank Pinkley (custodian)	1901
Mt. Rainier (WA)	1899	Oscar Brown (ranger)	1906
Crater Lake (OR)	1902	W. B. Arant (superintendent)	1902
Chickasaw (OK)	1902	Forest Townsley (patrolman)	1904
Wind Cave (SD)	1903	George Boland (forest ranger)	1903
Mesa Verde (CO)	1906	Charles Kelley (ranger)	1907
Devils Tower (WY)	1906	E. O. Fuller (custodian)	1908
Lassen Volcanic (CA)	1907	Lynne W. Collins (ranger-in-charge)	1922
Colorado (CO)	1911	John Otto (custodian)	1911
Rocky Mountain (CO)	1915	"Dixie" MacCracken (ranger)	1915
Sieur de Monts (Acadia) (ME)	1916	George B. Dorr (custodian)	1916
Hawaii (Volcanoes) (HI)	1916	Alex Lancaster (ranger)	1922
Mt. McKinley (Denali) (AK)	1917	Henry Karstens (ranger-at-large)	1921

NOTE: I am deeply indebted to both retired ranger John Henneberger, "professor emeritus," on the history of park rangers, as well as noted regional historian Shirley Sargent, author of *Protecting Paradise: Yosemite Rangers 1898–1960*, for their assistance on this section.

The First Rules and Regulations, April 19, 1877

The rules and regulations approved for Yellowstone National Park in 1877 seem simple compared to the many volumes governing national parks today. Although a step in the right direction, they were largely ineffective; the penalty attached to a violation was merely ejection from the park.

* * * *

All hunting, fishing or trapping within the limits of the park, except for the purpose of recreation to supply food for visitors or actual residents is strictly prohibited; and no sales, of fish or game taken from within the park, shall be made outside of its boundaries.

Persons residing within the Park or visiting it for any purpose whatever, are required, under severe penalties, to extinguish all fires which may be necessary to make, before leaving them. No fire must be made within the Park, except for necessary purposes.

No timber must be cut in the Park without a written permit from the Superintendent.

Breaking the siliceous or calcareous borders or deposits surrounding or in the vicinity of the springs or geysers for any purpose, and all removal, carrying away, or sale of specimens found within the Park, without the consent of the Superintendent is strictly prohibited.

No person shall be permitted to reside permanently within the limits of the Park without permission from the Department of the Interior and any person, now being within the Park, shall vacate the premises occupied by him within thirty days after having been served with a written notice to do so, by the Superintendent, or his deputy; said notice to be served upon him in person, or left at his place of residence.

Appointed a forest ranger for Sequoia National Park in December 1899, Britten assumed charge for the winter. Among his new duties was watching for poaching, even though he had no authority to arrest anyone; escorting the violator out was his only recourse. These long tours in the backcountry, up to thirty days, led to a divorce. In 1900 when the parks received their first congressionally appropriated money, Britten aided the army in building roads and minor infrastructure. As additional rangers were hired in successive years, Britten became the "park ranger in charge" or "chief ranger."

With the creation of the United States Forest Service in 1905, the seven rangers then working for these three California parks had to choose to either remain or go to the Forest Service. Ernest Britten was the only one to transfer into the newly formed agency and spent a combined twelve years in the parks and forest. He may have been the best of that early breed of men, reflecting the essence of what park rangers do today—protecting the resource while trying to accommodate ever-increasing numbers of visitors to the area.

Yellowstone rangers beginning a patrol in 1911. Back then skis were used more like snowshoes.
NATIONAL PARK SERVICE, HARPERS FERRY CENTER ARCHIVES

NATIONAL PARK
RANGER SERVICE

In 1915, the year before the National Park Service was created, the National Park *Ranger Service* was established by the Secretary of the Interior. At the time there were eleven national parks and eighteen national monuments, plus Casa Grande Ruins and Hot Springs Reservation. All these areas operated autonomously and answered only to the Department of the Interior. The new National Park Ranger Service was intended to bring these thirty-one areas "under one supervisory umbrella" to be directed by Mark Daniels, the General Superintendent of National Parks (a precursor to today's NPS Director). A professional landscape engineer first appointed in 1914, Daniels authored regulations governing and coordinating the ranger service. They were approved formally on January 9, 1915, by Interior Secretary Franklin Lane, and set forth the requirements for the position of ranger, the conditions for appointments and promotions, the organizational structure within a park, and the needed

National Register of Historic Places Plaque
Found at the 1907 Logging Ranger Station
in Glacier National Park

The first park rangers were chosen for their self-sufficiency and knowledge of backcountry travel. They were independent by nature and flourished in the splendid isolation of Glacier's wilderness. A good ranger was a jack-of-all-trades: part biologist, educator, fire fighter, trail and road builder, law enforcement officer, game warden, and general all-around handyman.

Winter was the most challenging season for the ranger. Frequent snowshoe patrols were conducted far from the main ranger station and often as many as 300 miles of trail were traveled each month. Small snowshoe cabins, stocked with provisions and firewood were scattered along patrol routes. Patrols were conducted in all kinds of weather in order to discourage illegal fur trapping and hunting. During patrols, communications with park headquarters was non-existent. The ranger had to be capable of handling any situation.

Today, park rangers must possess many of the same skills and characteristics of the early day rangers, but modern technology has, to the regret of many, changed the routine of the job forever.

Early day rangers were men with a wide variety of outdoor skills. Their duties were varied but much time was spent on backcountry patrol. Until the 1940s, rangers were also responsible for predatory control. Today, both men and women patrol the backcountry, and predators are protected as an important element of the natural environment.

The first National Park Service Chief Ranger's conference, held in Sequoia National Park January 15–19, 1926. Notice the wide variety of hat crowns as well as the round brassards on the right coat sleeves denoting the ranger's position.
NATIONAL PARK SERVICE, SEQUOIA NATIONAL PARK ARCHIVES

Registering automobiles as they entered Glacier was an important part of a ranger's job in 1918. Rangers even recorded the serial number of the vehicle's motor.
NATIONAL PARK SERVICE, GLACIER NATIONAL PARK ARCHIVES

written monthly reports. Daniels directed the Ranger Service only until December 10, 1915, when Robert B. Marshall replaced him.

In the National Park Ranger Service, chief rangers in the larger parks were to earn $1,500 per year, assistant chiefs could expect to make $1,350, a ranger first class was to be paid $1,200, and a ranger was allotted $900 yearly. The lowest ranger position was that of temporary. Rangers began at Grade 5 and could move up through Grade 10 (that of a chief ranger). Although organizational and administrative vestiges from the National Park Ranger Service still exist, the "agency" itself was short-lived, having been absorbed into the National Park Service when it was created on August 25, 1916.

*Ranger Wayne Replogle astride his "elkified"
motorcycle in Yellowstone in 1932. Still going
strong in 1960, Replogle was a supervisor with
the Service's smoke jumper unit out of West
Yellowstone.*

NATIONAL PARK SERVICE, YELLOWSTONE NATIONAL
PARK ARCHIVES

Chapter 4
SYMBOLS OF PROTECTION

THE RANGER BADGE

The National Park Service badge of today, worn by everyone in a standard uniform, is a gold shield. On it is represented a bison standing on grass and facing to the left in front of a background of mountains and a rising sun. In a circle around the edge of the badge are the raised words "U.S. Department of the Interior—March 3, 1849" (the date the Department of the Interior was established).

The first badge used in a national park was that of the "Yellowstone Park Scout." Created at the time of the Yellowstone Protection Act in 1894, the chief scout's sterling silver badge cost $1.25. Regular park scouts wore a badge made of German silver, which cost them 75 cents to replace. Ranger/scouts wore this mark of authority in Yellowstone until 1906, when it was replaced until 1913 by the "eagle" badge that depicted an eagle with open wings in the center of the seal of the Department of the Interior. The eagle was a prominent element in subsequent park service badges, including those worn by rangers until 1968.

It is not known what type of badge was issued to rangers in other parks during these early days. In one 1902 photograph from Sequoia, four men are shown,

The earliest known badge attributed to a national park is that of the "Yellowstone Park Scout," which probably came into use after the Lacey Act. Nickel-plated and two inches in diameter, it was worn from 1894 to 1906, when it was replaced by the "Eagle" badge.
NATIONAL PARK SERVICE, HARPERS FERRY CENTER ARCHIVES

This badge was worn by most rangers (except in Yellowstone) from 1906 to 1920. It was two inches in diameter and nickel-plated. Director Stephen Mather wore a similar badge that was gold rather than silver in color.
NATIONAL PARK SERVICE, HARPERS FERRY CENTER ARCHIVES

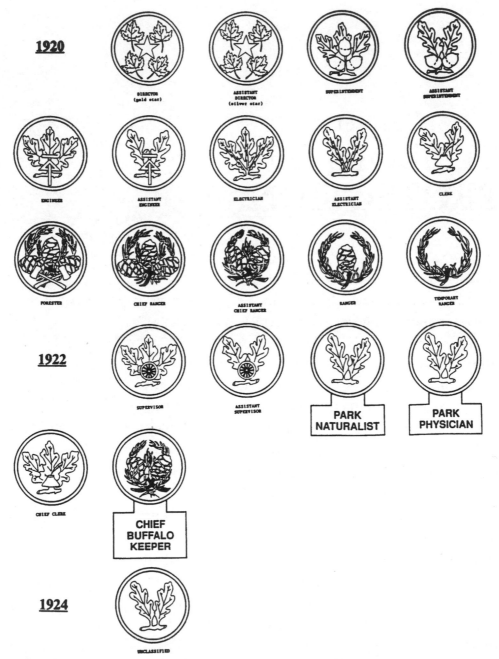

Authorized in 1920, brassards were 2¼ inches in diameter and worn on the uniform's right sleeve. There were three categories of brassards: directors, officers, and rangers. They were eliminated in 1934. <space>NATIONAL PARK SERVICE, HARPERS FERRY CENTER ARCHIVES</space>

From 1946 until 1960, all of these badges were used somewhere in the National Park Service. NATIONAL PARK SERVICE, HARPERS FERRY CENTER ARCHIVES

and each is wearing two different badges. One of the badges may have read "Forest Reserve Ranger," since at that time both the national parks and the forest reserves were managed by the Department of Interior. The forests later moved to the Department of Agriculture.

The first badge with the words "U.S. Park Ranger" on it was issued in 1920, and except for minor modifications such as the plating process, color, and some subtle variations in wording, it was used for the next forty years. It featured an eagle with outswept wings, its head facing to the left. During the 1930s all permanent National Park Service employees wore the same badge that the rangers did, a situation that was unpopular with the rangers.

In 1925 two designs for a park naturalist brassard were submitted to the service's first chief naturalist, Ansel Hall: a bird and a bear. NATIONAL PARK SERVICE, HARPERS FERRY CENTER ARCHIVES

From 1946 until 1960, half-dollar-sized round badges, either nickel or gold plated, replaced the traditional shield-shaped badges for all non-rangers.

Beginning in 1961, everyone in uniform wore the shield-shaped badge that read either "National Park Ranger" (for the superintendent and all rangers) or "National Park Service" (for everyone else). The park service regulation specified that "All uniformed employees except women, boat officers, and boat crews, lifeguards, nurses, and fire control aides will wear the shield badge." This apparently sexist limitation on the wearing of the badge

Issued in 1968, this badge displayed the "new" seal of the Department of Interior. It proved so unpopular that it was replaced two years later with the badge in use today. The department's old seal with the buffalo quickly returned.
NATIONAL PARK SERVICE, HARPERS FERRY CENTER ARCHIVES

by women had little impact in the ranger ranks; there were few females in uniform at the time.

A radical change to the badge was introduced in 1968. The Department of the Interior's buffalo seal was replaced by one depicting a small circle (symbolizing the sun), over two triangles (abstract mountains), over nine small triangles (representing water), all framed by a stylized pair of cupped hands. This was part of the Park Service's effort to incorporate a bit of the modern into its uniforms and symbols. The employees wearing the new design referred to it derogatorily as the "Good Hands" badge, in reference to the logo of a national insurance company.

There was such an outcry over these unpopular changes that within two years the Department of the Interior had restored the buffalo to its seal. At the same time, the National Park Service abandoned its use of the eagle symbol on the badge and adopted the Department of the Interior's buffalo with mountainous background, described above. By late 1969, a single badge had been developed to be worn by all National Park Service employees, and it is still in use today.

THE RANGER'S STETSON HAT

Nothing symbolizes the National Park Service more than a ranger in a "flat hat." Like a park ranger beginning a career, full of hope and expectation, his or her Stetson hat is new, clean, and fresh. By career's end, both have become veterans—frayed and worn by age and trial, but truly reflecting accomplishment and experience.

While camped near Colorado's Pikes Peak in 1862, John B. Stetson conceived the first of what would become his signature ranger hats. Soon thereafter he produced it, and then began marketing it the next year. With a rigid four-inch brim and pointed four-inch crown finished in fur, the "Boss of the Plains," as the original model was called, was perfect for both sun and rain. Not particularly becoming but functional in design, it quickly developed as a favorite

Ferdinand Castillo, here wearing the classic ranger Stetson in 1975, greeted visitors to Yosemite for nearly four decades from the same entrance station.
NATIONAL PARK SERVICE, YOSEMITE NATIONAL PARK RESEARCH LIBRARY

In 1928, a single uniform style was authorized for the service. Only superintendents, custodians, and rangers could wear badges as well as the round brassards worn on the sleeves.
NATIONAL PARK SERVICE, HARPERS FERRY CENTER ARCHIVES

of those working outdoors. That Stetson flat hat was the forerunner of the "campaign" hats later donned by our country's military, and also adopted in 1901 by the Royal Canadian Mounted Police.

In 1911 the Superintendent of Glacier National Park, Major William R. Logan, ordered uniforms for all fifteen of his rangers from an Eastern supplier. Each uniform consisted of "one Norfolk jacket, one wool shirt, one pair riding trousers, one pair leggings, and one felt camping hat after the Stetson style," and cost $15. Until then, the men in the few existing national park areas had little way to distinguish themselves from the people they were serving. In 1912 the original military-style campaign hat, made in an Army olive drab and called an "Alpine" hat, cost $2.50.

Seeking to standardize its national identity in 1920, the newly created National Park Service adopted a uniform policy that required a hat that was a "Stetson, either stiff or cardboard brim . . . belly color." ("Belly" was short for "Belgian Belly," and used to describe the handsome reddish buff color of the underfur of the Belgian hare from which many fine hats were then made.)

Although today's ranger uniform has undergone a variety of modifications, the original and distinctive felt "flat hat" remains largely unchanged. In 1959, however, a straw, summer-weight version of the Stetson was authorized for appropriate parks. The beloved tannish-gray fur original, now selling for more than sixty dollars, is at the heart of the ranger tradition, and park rangers take great pride in wearing the same hat throughout their careers, which often span several decades.

THE HATBAND

If you look closely at the cordovan hatband on a ranger's Stetson hat, you will notice that the thin strap of leather is adorned with the tooled foliage and cones of the sequoia tree. The band is secured on the left by chrome ring fasteners joined to sequoia cones of metal. The sequoia symbols were chosen because these ancient and imposing trees were and still are living cornerstones of three of our first four national parks: Sequoia, General Grant, and Yosemite. Originally proposed to be acorns, these raised cones have been manufactured in both silver and gold over the years.

The National Park Service "sequoia cone" emblem prior to the present arrowhead adopted in 1952.
NATIONAL PARK SERVICE, HARPERS FERRY CENTER ARCHIVES

"Are You a Forest Ranger?"

Park rangers are often confused with forest rangers. As uniformed federal employees, all rangers are proud stewards of our precious resources. The difference is that park rangers work for the National Park Service, an agency within the Department of the Interior, while forest rangers serve the Forest Service, a bureau of the Department of Agriculture. The responsibilities of the two organizations as set forth by Congress are very different, although there are basic custodial similarities.

Park rangers have a dual, narrowly focused mission of preserving the areas within their care while providing for people's enjoyment of them. Forest rangers, on the other hand, administer the forests with a broader emphasis that is designed to make the most use of an area's many resources, including tree harvesting, range management, livestock grazing, mining, watershed protection, care of wildlife, fishing, hunting, and other recreational uses.

Both park and forest rangers are vital to the natural and cultural health and wealth of this country; they fight fires, provide interpretation and education, enforce laws relative to resources and people, administer to the needs of the land, and professionally accommodate the general public in innumerable ways.

When the hatband was conceived in 1929, its front had a blank space where specific park names could be impressed. This plan was quickly abandoned, apparently, for a "USNPS" (United States National Park Service) has been embossed on the band since 1930.

THE ARROWHEAD

The National Park Service arrowhead, a symbol of land management professionalism, was authorized as the agency's official emblem by the Secretary of the Interior on July 20, 1951. It was first used on a park road sign, as well as a ranger uniform in September of the next year. Suggested in 1949 by Aubrey V. Neasham, a park service historian, the insignia was refined, then approved, and quickly came to epitomize "what the parks are all about." It is a "thread of tradition" that runs through every facet of the National Park Service's history of protecting and conserving our national parks.

The arrowhead was intended to represent several aspects of the mission of the National Park Service. Its shape and earth-brown background embody our nation's impressive cultural heritage exemplified in the parks by archeology and history. The bison and the sequoia tree (symbols from the first two national parks—Yellowstone and Sequoia) represent the diverse natural world of plants and animals included within the system. The snowcapped mountain and glacier portrayed on the insignia's horizon, and the white of the water in its right foreground, signify the all-important values of scenery and recreation.

The current arrowhead appeared in 1952 and was first used in park brochures and signs. Permanent employees received three patches for their uniforms as well as a seasonal one. They were embroidered on a non-sanforized material and could only be used on coats.
NATIONAL PARK SERVICE, HARPERS FERRY CENTER ARCHIVES

The National Park Service Arrowhead was registered as an official emblem of the agency on February 9, 1965, by the United States Patent Office. To avoid both the commercial and unseemly use of this icon, its use is strictly limited by federal law (18 U.S.C. 701 & 36 C.F.R. 11.1–3).

"Tex" Roley patrolling the roads of Yellowstone in 1930. This style uniform was adopted in 1928 for motorcycle rangers. Notice the badge on the cap and the brassard on the sleeve.
NATIONAL PARK SERVICE, HARPERS FERRY CENTER ARCHIVES

Chapter 5
CREATING THE NATIONAL PARK SERVICE

On August 25, 1916, President Woodrow Wilson signed the National Park Service Act. It stated that the mission of the service was:

> [T]o promote and regulate the use of the Federal areas known as national parks, monuments, and reservations hereinafter specified by such means and measures as conform to the fundamental purpose of the said parks, monuments, and reservations, which purpose is to conserve the scenery and the natural and historic objects and the wildlife therein and to provide for the enjoyment of the same in such manner and by such means as will leave them unimpaired for the enjoyment of future generations.

The brand new agency, placed within the Department of the Interior, brought together thirty-seven separate and diverse areas: fourteen national parks, twenty-one national monuments, the Hot Springs Reservation, and the Casa Grande Ruin. For the first time, such dissimilar areas as Alaska's Sitka National Monument, Oregon's Crater Lake National Park, and northern Arizona's remote Navajo National Monument were collected under the same umbrella for protection and management.

The creation of the National Park Service did not happen quickly. A highly politicized Congress resisted the move, fears of regulation by western ranchers and miners had to be dispelled, and even the decade-old U.S. Forest Service felt threatened, and its resistance had to be overcome.

Which Was the First National Park?

Flanked by seasonal rangers in this 1920 photo, Horace M. Albright (fourth from right, standing) was just twenty-nine years old when appointed superintendent of the world's first national park. The two motorcycle riders are Emmitt and Hollis Matthew.
NATIONAL PARK SERVICE, HARPERS FERRY CENTER ARCHIVES

Early in the nineteenth century, mineral-laden hot springs became valued, particularly in Europe, for their healing qualities. Hoping to protect and make them available to the public, the U.S. government set aside forty-seven hot springs gushing from a fault at the base of the Ouachita Mountains in the Arkansas Territory. On April 20, 1832, Hot Springs National Health and Recreation Center was established.

Some asserted that the establishment of this federal reservation represented the first time that a natural area had been set aside by our government for the common good of all Americans. Because the Hot Springs act pre-dated the creation of Yellowstone National Park by more than forty years, there are those who have called the reserve the first national park in the United States. But it was protected for an entirely different reason than was Yellowstone. The intent at Hot Springs was to assure preservation and equitable distribution of a singular, utilitarian resource, much like our present national forests.

Over the years, facilities sprang up within the reserve and around the waters, and by 1873 the city of Hot Springs had six elegant bathhouses and two dozen lodging spots, largely catering to the "rich and famous." Bathhouse Row was created, and still exists today. Who owned what in the town soon became a serious issue. The question was resolved by the courts in 1880. That same year, the area was dedicated as a "reservation" on June 16.

When Congress established the National Park Service in 1916, thirty-seven existing areas were made part of the new agency, including Hot Springs Reservation, which was specifically mentioned in the enabling law's language. It actually became a national park in 1921.

Despite being a very welcome member of the National Park System, historians and students of the subject do not consider Hot Springs the world's first national park.

In about 1910, four men began a labor of love to create the new bureau. They were J. Horace McFarland (a respected horticulturist and urban planner); Frederick Law Olmsted, Jr. (a noted Harvard-trained landscape architect and the son of the creator of New York City's Central Park); Stephen T. Mather (whose borax mining earned him millions and who became the first director of the National Park Service); and Horace M. Albright (a graduate of the University of California who became the second director).

Concerned about the proposed damming of Yosemite's Hetch Hetchy Valley for a supply of water for San Francisco, McFarland in May 1910 suggested to the Secretary of the Interior that the national parks needed "general, intelligent and logical supervision." Heeding the advice of his Secretary, President Howard Taft (in his comments to the Congress) advocated that parks be preserved for the public's "edification and recreation."

Olmsted observed that the parks were in poor condition and lacked coordinated leadership, suggesting that they were "mixed up and rather inefficient." To address his concern about the chaos, he toiled for at least five years crafting a statement of purpose as well as philosophical principles for the proposed park service. Olmsted's language was incorporated into the act that created the new agency and was signed into law by President Wilson in 1916.

The enabling legislation provided for a National Park Service director at $4,500 annually, an assistant director at $2,500, a chief clerk at $2,000, a draftsman at $1,800, a messenger at $600, and as many employees as needed, so long as the cost for the new agency did not exceed $19,500. Congress appropriated $500,000 for operation of the existing thirty-seven areas.

What Happened to the Second National Park?

Three years after Yellowstone was created (1872), the country's second national park came into existence. Mackinac Island National Park, which included a fort and was entrusted to the Secretary of War, was set aside for the "health, comfort, pleasure, benefit and enjoyment of the people" in 1875. Located in northern Lake Huron, the 1,000-acre park was championed by Michigan's Senator Thomas W. Ferry, who was born there. Indistinguishable from millions of other forested acres in the Great Lakes region, Mackinac Island lacked most of the qualities that we associate with a national park today. Not surprisingly, it was ceded back to the State of Michigan in 1895 when the army proposed to abandon the island's fort and leave the site without a caretaker. It is now a state park.

Besides Mackinac Island, there have been more than sixty different national park areas—encompassing approximately 290,000 acres in twenty-eight states—that have been added to and later removed from the national park system for a variety of reasons.

Museum at Many Glacier Campground, Glacier National Park, 1932. Note sign advertising "Nature Lectures." NATIONAL PARK SERVICE, GLACIER NATIONAL PARK ARCHIVES

Chapter 6
THE EVOLUTION OF INTERPRETATION

In 1871 John Muir, reveling in the grand beauty of Yosemite and the High Sierra, resolved that "I'll interpret the rocks, learn the language of flood, storm and the avalanche. I'll acquaint myself with the glaciers and wild gardens, and get as near the heart of the world as I can." His use of "interpret" to mean "to make understandable" in the context of the significance of national parks is often cited as the beginning of the term's eventual adoption by the National Park Service. Now interpretation encompasses the wide range of educational programs offered to park visitors throughout the system.

Even before our parklands were established by law, their splendor and worth were heralded by authorities of the day. Among early efforts to "interpret" national parks for others were *The Yosemite Guide-Book* of 1869 by J. D. Whitney, California State Geologist; soon-to-be-superintendent Nathaniel P. Langford's two-part article, "Wonders of the Yellowstone Region," which appeared in *Scribner's Monthly* in 1871; *In the Heart of the Sierras*, written in 1886 by James Mason Hutchings, an early Yosemite settler; and Frances Theodora Dana's *How to Know the Wild Flowers*, released in 1893.

A ranger in the 1930s giving a talk in Glacier National Park. By today's standards, these visitors are dressed more for an afternoon tea than a romp in the great outdoors.
NATIONAL PARK SERVICE, GLACIER NATIONAL PARK ARCHIVES

Philetus W. Norris, Yellowstone National Park's second superintendent, performed rudimentary interpretation soon after his arrival in 1877. Norris, however, was more interested in the infrastructure needs of the new area, and paid much more attention to building roads than to educating tourists. George L. Henderson, an early assistant superintendent for the park, gave education a much higher priority. A fifty-four-year-old widower when he arrived in May 1882, he was recognized as the authority on the wonders of Yellowstone within three years.

Keenly interested in factual accuracy and effective communications when dealing with the public, the well-educated Henderson was the first park employee within the United States to be referred to as a "park interpreter." During his more than twenty years in the area, the resourceful Henderson invented place names, erected signboards at natural curiosities, wrote informative newspaper articles, led interpretive tours, and entertained visitors by reciting poetry to them among the geysers.

The United States Army replaced Yellowstone's civilian staff in 1886, and energetic and often-bored soldiers were called upon to explain the park's novel natural features to the curious visitors. Troopers were instructed to give those who inquired what information they could, "always in a courteous manner." Not particularly scientific in nature, these early "geyser cone talks" supplemented the information that stagecoach drivers and other park quasi-guides were providing their guests, and were essentially the original national park interpretive programs.

In the mid-1890s on the east coast, pioneering naturalist Anna Botsford Comstock founded the nation's first nature-education program in New York. Quickly adopted by Cornell University, the concept of nature education was eventually embraced by more enlightened schools all across the country. Comstock went on to publish the *Handbook of Nature Study* in 1911; the book stayed in print in twenty-four editions through 1939. For her contributions to outdoor education, the League of Women Voters identified Comstock as one of the twelve greatest living women in 1923. Greatly admired, she was the most widely recognized leader of the nature movement of the time.

At the end of the nineteenth century, progressive hotel operators in Yellowstone recruited vacationing schoolteachers who, while performing their other more mundane summer duties, gave lectures and spirited talks about the features of the area. This trend toward field education was evolving in other parks as well. In Rocky Mountain, Enos Mills, local inn-keeper-turned-park-crusader, recognized that his "mountainous backyard" was priceless, and he passionately promoted the area.

Born in 1870, Mills was guiding visitors to the top of 14,255-foot Longs Peak by his late teens. Between 1889 and 1922 he distinguished himself as naturalist, author of fifteen books about nature, lecturer, advocate for parks and preserves, founder of the Trail School (an early environmental education program), and teacher. Young women employed in park hotels served in Mills' Trail School as nature guides, and in 1917, sisters Elizabeth and Esther Burnell became the first to pass an examination as "nature teachers." Thus certified by Rocky Mountain National Park, they were the first women designated as naturalists by the National Park Service. When he died unexpectedly in 1922, Enos Mills was remembered as the architect of the profession of interpretation as well as the "father" of Rocky Mountain National Park.

The Evolution of
Interpretation

In 1915, campfire programs were being given to travelers at then-isolated Mesa Verde National Park by Dr. Jesse Walters Fewkes. A noted anthropologist and ethnographer of the period, Dr. Fewkes was doing ground-breaking archeological work in the area for the Smithsonian Institution. Mesa Verde claims that these interpretive efforts were the first for the National Park Service. Four years later, in 1919, the University of California inaugurated field lectures in the meadows and forests of Yosemite; their topics included the region's Indians, natural history, and conservation, including John Muir's thoughts and philosophies about preservation.

National Park Service educational and interpretive efforts really blossomed at Yosemite and Yellowstone in 1920. While vacationing at Lake Tahoe the previous summer, Director Mather had been greatly impressed by the two University of California professors giving weekly programs about nature at the Fallen Leaf Lodge, a rustic hostelry. He persuaded Drs. Loye Miller and Harold Bryant to relocate their presentations to Yosemite the next summer. Once there, Dr. Bryant, educational director of the California Fish and Game Commission, established the Yosemite Free Nature Guide Service.

This inspirational new program included hikes, evening campfires, and lectures illustrated by moving pictures at Camp Curry. "The response has been so great," Bryant reported of the first season's activities, "that we are sure there will be sufficient demand not only to continue the work in Yosemite National Park but to extend it to other parks."

At Yellowstone, Superintendent Horace M. Albright appointed Ranger Milton P. Skinner to the position of park naturalist, the Service's first. He was perfect for the job, having long studied the region's geology and biology. To assist Skinner with his new duties in 1920, Albright also hired two seasonal rangers to provide field trips, lectures, and written materials on natural history topics for dissemination in the area. One of them was Isabel Bassett Wasson, the first woman to serve as a paid interpreter for the National Park Service. In the morning she worked behind the information desk, and then gave three different lectures, one in the afternoon, one in the early evening, and a later one around the traditional campfire. She made certain that each of her programs was different, as she had developed a following of engrossed visitors.

Park educational programs began to expand throughout the country. Rocky Mountain National Park opened an information office for visitors in 1921. Yosemite officials hired forty-year-old Enid Reeves Michael, the wife of the local postmaster, as a seasonal ranger-naturalist to assist a cynical Harold Bryant. Dr. Bryant believed the position should be filled by a man and "did not approve of women taking part." Mount Rainier hired Charles Landes, a Seattle biology teacher, as a seasonal ranger-naturalist, and in Glacier, a local naturalist initiated a nature guide service; under permit with the National Park Service he was allowed to charge a fee. He was replaced in 1922 by Montana State College professors who offered educational programs without charge.

On the west coast, U. S. Commissioner Walter Fry, formerly Sequoia National Park superintendent, distributed nature bulletins there in 1922. A year later he formed the Sequoia Nature Guide Service, established a tent museum, and led nature walks. On the lip of the Grand Canyon that same year, Chief Clerk Michael J. Harrison gave talks about his park at the stylish El Tovar Hotel. Zion and Crater Lake National Parks instituted interpretive offerings over the next few years, and in 1928, Rocky Mountain hired its first

"Campfire programs" given by uniformed park rangers have been the cornerstone of National Park Service interpretation since the early 1900s.
NATIONAL PARK SERVICE, GLACIER NATIONAL PARK ARCHIVES

The Evolution of
Interpretation

ranger-naturalist, a woman by the name of Margaret Fuller Boos, a Ph.D. from the University of Chicago.

To strengthen these budding interpretive efforts, Director Steve Mather made Ansel Hall chief naturalist of the National Park Service in 1923. As head of the service's Education Division working from the forestry school at the University of California at Berkeley, he provided much-needed oversight and coordination while formalizing new standards for park naturalists. In 1926, Hall began searching for qualified applicants:

> The duties of Ranger Naturalist require a full day's work each day—work entailing continual contact with the public. If you are not absolutely certain that you can maintain an attitude of enthusiasm and courtesy, please do not apply for work of this sort. . . . A Ranger Naturalist may have to talk to 1500 to 2000 persons; his lectures may be a part of a general entertainment program where his competitors will be Jazz music, comedy skits, or other such forms of amusement. (Barry Mackintosh, *Interpretation in the National Park Service: A Historical Perspective*, 1986)

In Fiscal Year 2000, 2,096 permanent and 2,333 seasonal National Park Service Interpreters provided 528,738 formal presentations, demonstrations, special events, educational programs, and related outreach services.

Many rangers from the "old-time" military tradition looked upon the new male ranger-naturalists as less than manly, calling them "pansy pickers" and "butterfly chasers." When Yellowstone Superintendent Albright began to hire women as ranger-naturalists after World War I, their male counterparts came to see them as threats to their futures.

To better train these people and professionalize the Service, Dr. Harold Bryant founded the Yosemite School of Field Natural History in 1925. Beginning as a six-week session and expanding to seven in 1933, this summer course was the National Park Service's first official training. Offered for $25 initially, the field school was attended by more women than men, even though the "fairer sex" couldn't be considered for positions with the agency. The reason given was that females "couldn't fight fires, rescue injured rock climbers, bury dead animals, or carry out police duties."

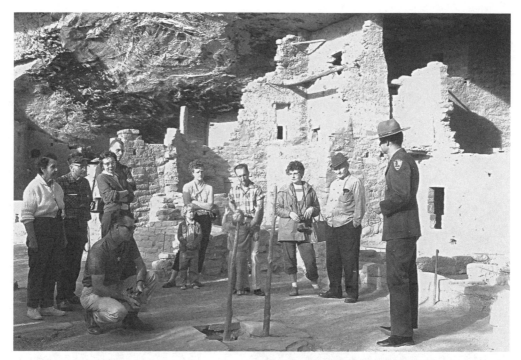

Education is the surest way to safeguard an irreplaceable resource. This ranger in Mesa Verde in 1959 is describing what life was like among these canyons hundreds of years ago.
NATIONAL PARK SERVICE, MESA VERDE NATIONAL PARK ARCHIVES

Limited to twenty students with at least two years of college, the program was devoted mostly to field work, distinguishing it from typical academic courses in the natural sciences. Upon earning their certificates, the new graduates vied for jobs in local parks and summer camps throughout the country. Hundreds of seasonal and permanent ranger-naturalists trained at the Yosemite Field School until it was finally discontinued in 1953. These naturalists served as the superintendent's "expert consultants on all matters pertaining to education and natural history" for decades. Park education for children began in Yosemite in 1930 with the establishment of the Junior Nature School, the antecedent of the service's present-day Junior Ranger Program.

The Evolution of
Interpretation

Seasonal ranger Pat Hill provides "living history" at Montana's Little Bighorn National Battlefield in the summer of 2000. General George Armstrong Custer and the 7th Cavalry clashed here with Sioux and Northern Cheyenne Indians in the famous 1876 battle.

In response to the country's burgeoning love affair with the car, guided auto caravans were introduced in Mesa Verde and Yosemite in 1929. The following year, uniformed park rangers led long lines of vehicles at Yellowstone, Grand Canyon, and Sequoia. Great crowd pleasers for the next decade, these parades of what John Muir once referred to as "blunt-nosed mechanical beetles" were common. Long queues of drivers would wend their way along park roads, often with the ranger at the front of the formation extolling the virtues of these beautiful areas through a rooftop loudspeaker. Increasing traffic and associated congestion eventually forced the discontinuance of the practice, although visitors still approximate the experience through the use of ever-popular, self-guided, auto audio programs.

An electric map, with colored lights highlighting various military actions, was in use at Vicksburg National Military Park in the early 1940s, and the Washington Monument used a recorded interpretive message for visitors beginning in 1947.

A number of educational archetypes were created in the 1930s. One of the country's first wayside exhibit shelters for interpreting the landscape was built (from native stone and logs to blend in with the environment) in 1931 at Yellowstone's Obsidian Cliffs; the structure is now listed on the National Register of Historic Places. For a short time in 1932, park naturalists (on an experimental basis) accompanied private airplane tour flights over the Grand Canyon as well as on deep-sea fishing excursions off Acadia National Park on the coast of Maine. Always open to innovation, Glacier National Park interpreters boarded a cross-country train in East Glacier for the hour-long trip to West Glacier. As they meandered along the southern boundary of the spectacular Montana park, rangers in the 1970s pointed out highlights of the area to the passengers.

HISTORIANS

Historical parks, such as Mississippi's Tupelo National Battlefield or Lincoln's Home in Illinois, seem to demand more explanation and narrative than natural and recreational areas do. The National Park Service's responsibility with these keepsakes is to aid in the appreciation of our heritage by fostering an understanding of our past.

In 1931, the agency's first two field historians, Floyd Flickinger and Elbert Cox, were hired by William Robinson, a progressive superintendent at

Colonial National Monument. Several months later Director Albright appointed Verne E. Chatelain, chairman of the history and social sciences department at Nebraska State Teachers College, as chief historian for the service. In 1933 Chatelain wrote that "the sum total of the sites which we select [for the system] should make it possible for us to tell a more or less complete story of American History." Other early NPS historians included Sallie P. Harris, hired in the winter of 1934 at Arizona's Montezuma Castle to classify artifacts from a dig, and Jean McWhirt Pinkley, who began in 1939 as an archeologist at Mesa Verde and enjoyed a career that spanned thirty years.

Over the coming three decades, seventy-one historic (and prehistoric) areas came to be included in the National Park System, largely through the Historic Sites Act of 1935. Signed into law on August 21, it established "a national policy to preserve for public use historic sites, buildings and objects of national significance for the inspiration and benefit of the people of the United States." Such seemingly diverse places as the 694-mile-long Natchez Trace Parkway, the Thomas Jefferson Memorial on the pedestrian mall of our nation's capital, and Florida's isolated Fort Jefferson National Monument (now Dry Tortugas National Park) came into being. The act also provided for museums, for an in-depth educational program, and for the erection and maintenance of "tablets to mark or commemorate historic or prehistoric places and events of national historical or archaeological significance."

Many areas within the system, even those set aside for their natural resources (such as Carlsbad Caverns National Park), have professional historians on staff. Today there are approximately two hundred practicing historians within the National Park Service.

> Stephen Mather encouraged construction of golf courses in Yosemite and Yellowstone, believing that tourists would stay longer in the parks if they had more to entertain them.

PARK MUSEUMS

In 1904, Yosemite's Acting Superintendent, hoping to learn more about the area that he managed, asked the Secretary of Agriculture to provide books and publications dealing with the natural history of the area. As the importance of park flora and fauna became more appreciated, steps were taken to emphasize and showcase these natural resources. In the south end of the park, one hundred acres were selected for a botanical garden; trees were trimmed, underbrush

Fred Jeep, a local living near Mesa Verde National Park in 1916, holds an ancient clay pot. Within the year, this artifact was housed in the park's new museum, one of the service's earliest. FRED JEEP HISTORICAL COLLECTION, MESA VERDE NATIONAL PARK ARCHIVES

and debris were removed, and short trails were built. Amateur naturalist Dr. Henry F. Pipes, a military surgeon then in the park, labeled three dozen different plants along these forested pathways. It was hoped that this garden would someday be "supplemented by a building serving the purpose of a museum and library." When Lt. Pipes discovered that all his pioneering work lay on private land, the park's newborn interpretive efforts were abandoned.

Ranger Terry Brown at Philadelphia's Independence Hall provides directions to a park visitor in 1999. CLARK GUY COLLECTION

One of the first "museum exhibits" in a park was established the following year, when Frank "Boss" Pinkley, first custodian of Arizona's Casa Grande Ruins, began displaying ancient artifacts recovered nearby. As early as 1908, officials at Yellowstone had requested that information on the park's geology, plants, and animals

The Evolution of
Interpretation

Rangers in the White House

Undoubtedly, 1600 Pennsylvania Avenue is the most famous address in the United States. Most people are surprised to learn that many National Park Service rangers and other employees work there daily. Oversight of the Executive Mansion was transferred to the NPS in 1933, and park personnel have provided a variety of services to White House visitors ever since.

Development of the White House was made possible when on July 16, 1790, President George Washington approved legislation creating the District of Columbia and authorizing the purchase of lands for federal buildings. The following year he chose the site of the capital near his home at Mount Vernon and acquired seventeen different reservations. Reservation 1 became the site of the White House, Lafayette Park, and the Ellipse; Reservation 2 was designated the site for the Capitol; and the Washington Monument was eventually built on Reservation 3.

A symbol of freedom, the White House, sitting on eighteen acres of grounds, is the oldest public building in the District of Columbia and has served as both the residence and office of the President of the United States since November 1, 1800. Its cornerstone, on a foundation dug by slaves, was laid October 13, 1792. Largely destroyed by the British in 1812, it was rebuilt two years later and was the largest house in the United States until after the Civil War. Until 1901 when Teddy Roosevelt officially changed its name, the White House was known generally as the Executive Mansion or the President's House.

Today, the National Park Service provides many services at the facility, including ranger-led tours, landscaping, maintenance, and general administration. Special events at the White House are coordinated by the service also, with such annual highlights as the Easter Egg Roll, the lighting of the National Christmas Tree, and the Christmas Pageant of Peace among them. Besides numerous foreign dignitaries, over 1.5 million members of the public visit the grounds annually and hear interpretive talks provided by park rangers. Tours inside the White House are conducted by the United States Secret Service.

In 2001, the National Park Service budget for administering the White House was $6,936,000, with approximately seventy people staffing the area at peak season. In addition to the National Park Service, there are ten other agencies sharing stewardship of the White House.

be furnished for the "better education and information" of the protectors of the area. In 1913, Lieutenant Colonel L. M. Brett, Acting Superintendent of Yellowstone, called the attention of the Secretary of the Interior to the "necessity for an administration building, housing all that is interesting in historical data and specimens of natural curiosities, etc."

In 1917, a ranger station was converted at Mesa Verde National Park for museum purposes, and five exhibit cases were installed. The next year they

Yosemite Chief Ranger Forest Townsley (left), with two unidentified men, poses with two bloodhounds in this 1924 photo. Notice the "Bureau of Information" sign in the background.
MRS. JOHN BINGAMAN COLLECTION

displayed Anasazi bones, cultural relics, and photos of the park's ruins. Dr. Jesse Walter Fewkes, a Smithsonian scientist and early expert on Hopi Kachinas and the Indians of the Southwest, lectured on his extensive pre-historic cultural work in the park.

Milton Skinner started Yellowstone's park museum in 1920 in a former bachelor officer's quarters at Mammoth Hot Springs. The building still functions as a museum and information center. Skinner's exhibits included animal specimens prepared by the park's Chief Ranger, Sam T. Woodring. The same year, Ranger Ansel F. Hall organized the Yosemite Museum Association to plan and raise funds for a new park museum. He converted a former studio of a local artist to this purpose. Containing six rooms of displays designated for history, ethnology, and natural history, it highlighted a three-dimensional scale model of Yosemite Valley built by Hall. "He used a jigsaw, cardboard, modeling clay, and 25 pounds of brads" (Barry Mackintosh, *Interpretation in the National Park Service: A Historical Perspective*, 1986). When the museum opened in June 1922, visitors could view stuffed animals prepared by Chief Ranger Forest Townsley.

The Evolution of
Interpretation

Director Mather's 1920 annual report to the Secretary of the Interior called for "the early establishment of adequate museums in every one of our parks" to highlight the natural history of the diverse regions in the system. There was no federal money for this purpose, however. The government finally funded a museum—the Sinnott Memorial on the rim high above Crater Lake—in 1930. Even then, the Carnegie Foundation paid for its exhibits and equipment.

Those park museums established in Yosemite, Yellowstone, Grand Canyon, Lassen, and Mesa Verde between 1924 and 1930 were built through the philanthropic support of individuals and foundations. With money from private sources, the NPS was able to exhibit local plants and animals, promote scientific investigation, build research libraries, study area ethnography, and disseminate information on the park's natural and human history. During the 1930s, many historians—"historical technicians"—were hired with Civilian Conservation Corps money to conduct research for exhibits and site development, prepare publications, and give talks and tours for the public. In 1935 the Service established a Museum Division at the national level, and seventy-six museums were operating within the system by 1939.

NOTE

My thanks to National Park Service historian Barry Mackintosh (retired) and his 1986 book, *Interpretation in the National Park Service: A Historical Perspective,* for much of the information in the historians section.

Chapter 7
EARLY YEARS OF
RESOURCE MANAGEMENT

*The history of America has been the story of
Americans seizing, using, squandering and be-
latedly protecting their natural heritage.*
—President John F. Kennedy, 1963

In establishing Yellowstone in 1872, Congress directed
that the world's first national park should be retained in
a "natural condition." The enabling act forbade the "wanton destruction of the fish and game" while also providing
for "preservation, from injury or spoliation, of all timber,
mineral deposits, natural curiosities, or wonders." With these brief phrases the
underpinnings were laid for preserving our country's natural and cultural resources; decades would pass before most would come to appreciate the impli-
cations for conservation in the United States that they held.

By 1900 only five national parks had been set aside by the federal government. As vote-conscious politicians slowly came to recognize the economic
potential of tourism, the move to protect large tracts of the West for the greater
good began to gain momentum. For many, the riches of Yellowstone, Sequoia,
General Grant, Yosemite, and Mount Rainier embodied our country's once
seemingly limitless resources. As the system of national parks grew, managing
these lands, their wildlife, and their cultural treasures became a significant administrative challenge.

A legislative landmark, the 1906 Antiquities Act (aimed at preventing
"pot hunting" and related archeological looting) authorized the president "to
declare by public proclamation historic landmarks, historic and prehistoric

A ranger's first duty is to protect the resource. In this 1975 photo in Sequoia National Park, hikers and riding stock have seriously harmed a backcountry meadow. This trail will be closed and then rerouted around the fragile area. NATIONAL PARK SERVICE, SEQUOIA NATIONAL PARK ARCHIVES

structures, and other objects of historic or scientific interest" located on lands under control of the federal government to be national monuments. Wyoming's 865-foot-high Devils Tower, New Mexico's El Morro, and Arizona's Montezuma Castle were the first three areas to be formally recognized for such qualities. These sites and others like them were typically located in remote places, were overlooked by the public and largely inaccessible for tourism, and were neglected for years.

These first parks and monuments were administered as expanses of wilderness and beauty, they were kept free of fires, and their animals were protected. Unfortunately, their ecological well-being was generally measured by their physical attractiveness from a scenic perspective. The use of applied science and biological research was unheard of, so the definition and management of "natural conditions" varied from one superintendent to the next.

Early park managers and rangers took two basic approaches to managing the natural resources of the treasures in their care: they ignored them or they manipulated them. Because so little was known about science- and research-based preservation, the killing of predators, fish stocking, regulating animal populations, fighting forest fires, and eradicating diseased trees were practices at the core of early natural resource management.

Scientific method was slowly introduced to the parks. In 1927, Yosemite set aside seven square miles of high mountain country north of Tuolumne Meadows for purposes of study. Titled a Research Reserve, it was the first of an eventual twenty-eight such scientific spots in the Park System. Other areas existed in Zion, Glacier, and Sequoia.

At a 1929 conference, park naturalists noted that scientific information about their parks was "almost infinitesimal." That summer, a survey of park wildlife System-wide was initiated and privately funded by University of California-trained George M. Wright, twenty-five years old, independently wealthy, and Yosemite's Assistant Chief Naturalist. Conceptually supported by Director Albright, this was the Service's first scientific study of natural resources. In July 1931, the NPS assumed half the survey costs, with the other half still funded by Wright. This cost sharing lasted for two more years, when Albright finally established the Wildlife Division of the National Park Service with Wright as its head.

Wright's field survey resulted in *Fauna of the National Parks of the United States: A Preliminary Survey of Faunal Relations in National Parks*, released in 1932. A milestone work commonly known as "Fauna No. 1," its recommendations were unprecedented. They proposed the perpetuation of existing natural conditions and, if possible, the return of each park to a truly natural state, radical departures from the practices managers and rangers had been following. The director adopted Fauna No. 1 as policy in 1934 and urged park superintendents to appoint field rangers (preferably those with "some biological training and native interest in the subject") to coordinate wildlife management.

Soon rangers were being trained whenever possible for conducting a "continual fish and game study program" and for assisting the few biologists then in the service. Many of these new "wildlife rangers" found these innovative practices completely at odds with their long-established routines such as predator control, mosquito abatement, fire fighting, and stocking park waters with fish.

In 1934, ranger Ben Thompson, one of the first four wildlife biologists in the NPS, declared that no "first or second class nature sanctuaries are to be found in any of our national parks under their present condition." He noted that . . .

Two rangers prepare for a patrol in the Yosemite backcountry, circa 1925. Notice the pistol slung on the hip of Forest Townsley on the left.
NATIONAL PARK SERVICE, YOSEMITE NATIONAL PARK RESEARCH LIBRARY

white tail deer, cougar, wolf, lynx, and perhaps wolverine and fisher, were most likely "gone from the Yellowstone fauna." The Rocky Mountain National Park carnivore situation was much the same, except that it had also lost its grizzly population. At Grand Canyon feral burros had "decimated every available bit of range" in the canyon, and domestic livestock had taken a "heavy toll from the narrow strip of South Rim range." Moreover, Grand Canyon's cougars were "almost extirpated," and bighorn sheep were greatly reduced, while the "entire ground cover and food supply for ground dwelling birds and small mammals had been altered by cattle grazing." Yosemite National Park had lost its bighorn and grizzly populations and its cougars were "almost gone." In Glacier the grizzly were "very scarce." The trumpeter swan and bison were missing, and game species in general were "seriously depleted because of inadequate boundaries."

Predator control, such as the killing of mountain lions by professional hunters in Sequoia National Park in the 1920s, was official policy in the national parks until 1934. The park's superintendent, John R. White, is on the far right.
NATIONAL PARK SERVICE, SEQUOIA NATIONAL PARK ARCHIVES

A unique trait of most of the early large parks was an extensive, protected, and "wild" backcountry. With modern encroachments such as hotels, roads, campgrounds, and other facilities impacting only certain areas, the great majority of the park and its resources were escaping brutal overuse by people. But was it too late?

PREDATOR CONTROL

Among the early resource management efforts by managers of our country's parks and forests, one of the most questionable and least "scientific" (in retrospect) was the intentional, systematic elimination of large predators from the natural scene. Although we now understand the harm caused by this biological tampering, aggressive predator control was a well-accepted resource-management principle during the first half of the twentieth century.

The first parks were valued for their scenery; the prospect of seeing spectacular wildlife also enticed people to visit. The more "charming" animals such as elk, deer, bighorn sheep, mountain goats, and antelope were definitely favored over the mammals that preyed on them. For example, a 1906 military circular authorized non-commissioned officers in charge of Yellowstone soldier stations to kill mountain lions, coyotes, and wolves. Yellowstone's superintendent, Horace M. Albright, reflected the bias against these species when he defined predators as those mammals that preyed on "animals that add so much to the pleasure of park visitors."

In 1929, Assistant Director Albright led an aggressive campaign to host the 1932 Winter Olympics in Yosemite National Park. It lost out to Lake Placid, New York. As it turned out, Lake Placid suffered from a dearth of natural snow during the Olympics while Yosemite was inundated.

Both the army and park rangers hunted and killed these animals with great thoroughness. In 1915, the newly established Bureau of Biological Survey also began an extermination campaign against the meat eaters. Besides the rangers (who often augmented their salaries through the sale of the skins of the animals they killed), hired professional hunters also reduced the predator populations through shooting, trapping, poisoning, and tracking with dogs. These practices were so effective that mountain lions, coyotes, and wolves became extinct in Glacier, Yellowstone, and Rocky Mountain National Parks by the mid-1920s.

Other meat eaters on the hunters' "hit list" included coyotes, lynx, porcupines, bobcat, fox, badger, mink, weasel, fisher, otter, and marten. Not even predators of trout were immune. For a time during the 1920s, Albright's rangers destroyed the eggs of the fish-eating pelican and eliminated lake otters, to protect the trout and improve local fishing.

Steel traps were still being used at the Grand Canyon into the early 1930s, although by that time most of the carnivores were being "merely reduced" and not completely eliminated. On November 12, 1934, after years of watching park habitats increasingly degrade, the highly devastating and regrettable era of predator control in our national parks ended by official order of the director of the National Park Service.

A ranger stocks fingerlings in Glacier's remote Logging Lake in 1943. From at least the early 1880s, countless numbers of fish have been planted in park lakes. Even today, park managers must deal with the negative consequences of this long-abolished policy.
NATIONAL PARK SERVICE, GLACIER NATIONAL PARK ARCHIVES

FISH STOCKING

The single most extensive manipulation of wildlife undertaken by the National Park Service over the years was its management of fish populations. Artificial stocking of park lakes with fish—both native and non-native species—had begun by 1881, when sportfishing was first enhanced for tourists in Yellowstone. These initial efforts led to other stocking programs that were supported by hatchery operations both inside and outside the park's boundaries. Between 1894 and 1918, the military stocked the crystal waters of Yellowstone National Park with over nine million game fish.

Elsewhere in the parks, similar fishery management was begun. Fourteen years before Crater Lake was set aside as a park (1888), the state of Oregon had initiated fish stocking there. By the mid-1920s, fish hatcheries had been built in Glacier, Mt. Rainier, and Yosemite, and two more were later erected in Yellowstone. In 1922 alone, Yellowstone planted more than one million trout fingerlings and almost 7.4 million fry and eyed eggs. More than 125,000 Loch

Early Years of
Resource Management

Leven trout were planted in Bright Angel Creek of the Grand Canyon in 1925, and the next year 3.3 million trout fry, all from the local hatchery, were planted in Glacier.

Despite a resolution in 1921 by the Ecological Society of America to "strictly forbid" the introduction of non-native plants and animals, many of these restricted fish found their way into national park waters. Lugged in metal milk cans on the backs of both men and mules into remote locations, such fish were planted in large numbers even before many areas were set aside as parks. While they did provide improved recreation opportunities for fishermen, they caused eventual consternation for the rangers who understood that ecological disasters were in the making.

In 1936 Director Arno Cammerer issued the agency's first written fish management policy: non-native species were not to be introduced in waters where only native fish existed, and in waters where exotic and native fish both existed, the native species were to be "definitely encouraged." In 1939 the National Park Service established the policy that fishing was acceptable because of its "readily replaceable nature" and because the sport resulted in "recreational benefits far outweighing any possible impairment of natural conditions." That policy is still in effect today, and constitutes the only "taking" of wildlife permitted in the national parks, albeit completely inconsistent with other wildlife policies.

This safety message is handed out at every entrance station in Yellowstone. Protecting the visitor while safeguarding park resources is paramount to the ranger.
NATIONAL PARK SERVICE, YELLOWSTONE NATIONAL PARK ARCHIVES

BISON RANCHING

There were seventy-five million American bison, commonly called buffalo, when Europeans arrived, as estimated by Naturalist Ernest Thompson Seton. In 1884, the largest single remaining group of wild bison left in the United States was in Yellowstone National Park. With the Yellowstone herd dwindled to about two hundred, and a year after a notorious bison poaching incident and subsequent articles in *Forest and Stream*, President Grover Cleveland signed a law protecting the species on May 7, 1894. At the time, the Yellowstone Protection Bill finally

During this buffalo reduction in Yellowstone, 397 animals were removed and donated to nearby Native Americans. On horseback in this 1944 photo are buffalo herder Jim Kimberlin, pack master Paul Hoppe, and ranger Bob Murphy. BOB MURPHY COLLECTION

gave national park officials authority to arrest and prosecute illegal hunters. But change came too late; in 1895 Seton concluded there were only eight hundred of these majestic animals left in all the world, the vast majority on private ranches and game farms.

In the early years, park management practiced buffalo roundups, winter feeding, shipping surplus animals to zoos and preserves, castrating young bulls, inoculating against disease, and the culling of aged and sick animals. On occasion during the 1920s, honored park guests were even treated to the sight of bison stampedes. Killing buffalo within the park—certainly more controversial today than in the early years—first began in 1925 when National Park Service Director Stephen Mather permitted seventeen of Yellowstone's animals to be shot in conjunction with a local summer celebration.

Yellowstone's first attempt at "corralling" the buffalo began in 1895; it proved unsuccessful. Hoping to avoid extinction of the species, the park began "buffalo ranching" in 1902, with only twenty-two animals counted in the wild population that year. Until 1952, Yellowstone maintained Buffalo Ranch in the Lamar Valley with a chief buffalo keeper, an assistant, two herders, and an irrigator for the five hundred to eight hundred tons of hay being grown on six hundred acres of farmed parkland. Animals were allowed to roam "free" during the months when natural forage was available, with many of them then being rounded up and corralled at the ranch during the park's hostile winter.

Numbering about twenty-five hundred today, the Yellowstone buffalo herd is the last free-roaming group in the United States.

FOREST FIRE SUPPRESSION

Organized efforts to contend with forest fire in this country began as early as 1743, when New York adopted a statute giving officials authority to enlist citizens to fight local wildfires. Rudimentary fire protection initiatives were undertaken by the "Division of Forestry" of the Department of Agriculture in the 1880s, but forest fire protection by the federal government really began in Yellowstone National Park in 1886.

The Army assumed administrative control of Yellowstone that summer, with small detachments garrisoned at fifteen stations throughout the park. Congress, in its annual report on Yellowstone National Park for 1886, stated that "The most important duty of the superintendent and assistants in the park is to protect the forests from fire and ax." Taking this to heart, Captain Moses Harris, the park's first military superintendent (and a Congressional Medal of Honor recipient), soon began to fight fires, developing roads, trails, and communication networks to assist in this enterprise.

Until that time, "sage-brushing," as camping was known, was permitted almost anywhere in the park and tourists often left their campfires unattended. Some effort was made to control these fires, but the park had little staff. Some fires were even set by corrupt frontiersmen, both to embarrass the civilian administration and to drive animals into the open for easier hunting. Park workers battled over one hundred fires in 1888 (they burned a total of only five acres of parkland); another sixty-one were extinguished the next year. To outfit his employees for fire fighting duty, the superintendent asked his superiors in Washington for twenty axes and twenty rubber buckets. When this request went unanswered, a tourist from Pennsylvania bought them for the park. To limit the hazard of fires from campers, the Army established the first formal campgrounds in Yellowstone in 1889–1890 and forbade camping outside these designated areas.

In California, John Muir raged against wanton fires, particularly those set by herders of sheep and cattle in the Sierra. Stephen Mather, the agency's first director, called fire the "forest fiend," and the National Park Service generally embraced the Forest Service's total suppression policy. Rapid and broad attack on fires in the parks became a primary objective, and the elimination of wildland fire was established as a sacrosanct NPS policy. Park managers compared the scenic resources of parks to "priceless pieces of art" that should not be endangered by fire. Some went so far as to advocate that the agency should have the most efficient fire control organization in the country.

It was not until 1922, however, that the National Park Service received a special appropriation for fire control (it totaled $10,000). Not long thereafter, a major wildfire in Glacier in 1926 forced the service to create its first office at the national level solely devoted to natural resource management. This new "division of forestry" was initially overseen by Ansel F. Hall, the agency's first chief naturalist, who had been trained as a forester. In the summer of 1928, Hall hired John Coffman from the U. S. Forest Service, and Hall's division was renamed "education and forestry." The two men developed the first written NPS fire policy, adopted in 1931: to provide for the "prevention, detection and suppression" of fires; cooperate with other agencies with lands near parks; execute removal of potential fire hazards; train firefighters; and establish a fire reporting and review process.

PRESCRIBED FIRE

Although Native Americans often ignited fires for their beneficial effects on the land, Europeans didn't do so until the 1880s. Such fires, which reduced fuel hazards around buildings and maintained open meadows for ungulates, were recognized as wise forest management by a few advanced thinkers. Unfortunately, few in the National Park Service saw the value of letting fire burn in appropriate situations.

During World War II, the cause of preventing wild fires became a patriotic one, and the U. S. Forest Service joined the National Advertising Council in developing promotional materials to encourage fire awareness. On August 9, 1944, a smiling Smokey Bear wearing a ranger hat was introduced to the world as a symbol for fire prevention. Later, a real-life black bear was "found" orphaned following a catastrophic forest fire in New Mexico, quickly given the name Smokey, and the legend of the anti-fire bruin was created.

The first effort to study the positive effects of fire in the national parks was initiated in the Everglades in 1951. Conducted by biologist William B. Robertson, Jr., the studies that followed led to National Park Service experiments in 1958 that would become known as prescribed burning: selected natural and human-caused fires that were allowed to burn in ways simulating natural conditions. The following year, Sequoia National Park's ecologist Richard Hartesveldt issued a report indicating that California's giant sequoia trees needed fire, both to clear away abnormal accumulations of fuel at their bases and to help germinate their seeds. There are stories that Sequoia Chief Ranger Pete Schuft drove along park roads at the time throwing lighted matches out of his green government truck, hoping to reintroduce the natural fire lost to the ecosystem for decades.

The 1960s saw prescribed and natural fire gradually gain acceptance by land management agencies and the general public. With the enactment of the 1964 Wilderness Act and the setting aside of many millions of acres, the blanket policy of strict fire suppression had to be reconsidered. Fire had come to be seen as a natural phenomenon, with an important role in the ecology of national parks. The many years of regarding "fire as a fiend" had to be undone.

Changing attitudes about fire was not simple, particularly because people increasingly chose to live in forests and near underbrush. The job of managing fire in parks that adjoined urban and developed areas became more difficult and controversial. During the 1960s and 1970s, several areas, such as Arizona's Saguaro and New Mexico's Bandelier National Monuments, were testing grounds in the country's much-needed and ultimately successful prescribed fire program.

Despite the May 2000, tragedy—in which nearly fifty thousand acres in northern New Mexico and at least 220 homes in Los Alamos were consumed as a result of a National Park Service prescribed fire that got out of hand—fire is absolutely critical to the ecological health of this country's wildlands and to the safety of those who choose to live near them.

BEAR SHOWS

The evolution of agency-sanctioned "bear shows" in several parks can be traced back to the nightly disposal of food scraps and kitchen garbage at the early Yellowstone inns. At the park's first hotel—Sarah and George Marshall's 1880 log structure near the Lower Geyser Basin—a bear broke into the storeroom in the spring of 1881, seemingly attracted by the odors of an "easy" meal. Mrs. Marshall shot and killed the four-legged intruder.

Feeding shows like this one in Sequoia's "Bear Pit" during the 1930s were encouraged until the eve of World War II.

NATIONAL PARK SERVICE, SEQUOIA NATIONAL PARK ARCHIVES

Seventeen years later, a tourist at the Fountain Hotel noted that "from ten to sixteen bears came there for their supper, 'quietly munching the bones and fruit peelings, while a dozen or two of the hotel guests look on ten yards away'." One of the duties of a Yellowstone soldier in the early 1900s was to serve as "bear guard." The Army supervised the feeding of these animals near the hotels, the men often remaining at their posts until 9 P.M.

Officially prohibited in 1902, the roadside hand-feeding of bears and other animals was tacitly allowed for many years. During the first four decades of the twentieth century, the Service intentionally brought bears and people together with advertised nightly shows at some garbage dumps. In Sequoia's

Early Years of
Resource Management

Rangers transplant a tranquilized bear out of the Two Medicine area of Glacier in 1969. Since the park was established in 1910 fewer than a dozen people have been killed by grizzly bears. Left to right are Dave Shea, Bud Izzler, J. D. Young, Walt Wilking, and Bob Frauson.
AL NELSON PHOTO

Giant Forest, tourists gathered after dark at "Bear Hill" to watch the animals root through trash left for the occasion.

During the same era, officials flood-lit an arena west of Yosemite's Old Village and fed black bears for an excited gathering of tourists and residents alike. "It was the social event of the evening." Often as many as eight hundred vehicles lined the road near the site; 16,400 people attended the program in June 1930. These wildlife carnivals became so notorious in a few areas that armed rangers were assigned to protect fascinated crowds from grizzly bears and the more numerous but equally unpredictable black bears.

As a public service in Yellowstone, bear feeding was restricted in the 1930s to just one area, Canyon. On July 4, 1936, sitting behind a chain link fence on a hillside overlooking an elaborate concrete feeding platform, 2,476 people looked on. On August 6 of the following year, "seventy grizzlies and seven black bears foraged there on hotel garbage" at one time. Finally, under specific orders from the National Park Service director and with a ranger work force drastically eroded by the demands of war, park managers halted the shows in the summer of 1942. Unnatural attractions such as Bear Hill soon turned "garbage-hungry bears loose in the campgrounds to the dismay of rangers and visitors."

The National Park Service now pays strict heed to scientists, striving to separate animals from people. That segregation has yet to be achieved . . . and it may never be. Roadside "bear jams" (and other animals) still occur as innocent creatures beg for easy food and clueless visitors want to have photos taken with the seemingly "tame" animals.

SOME OTHER EARLY
RESOURCE MANIPULATIONS

- In the early years, rangers focused on maintaining those plants and animals that most visitors seemed to enjoy, and the NPS "ranched and farmed" the favored species. Those that threatened the more attractive wildlife were destroyed. Less visible life forms, such as small mammals, were of little concern to park administrators and largely ignored.

- To avert starvation of park mammals when harsh Yellowstone winters made finding food difficult, the Army began to feed elk, antelope, deer, and bighorn sheep in 1904, with up to fifteen hundred tons of hay being provided to those animals by 1919. Similar supplemental feedings for ungulates were carried out in other western parks during this period.

- Assisted by local hunters, Yellowstone rangers began harvesting elk in January 1935, after determining that there were too many animals and that their habitat was being seriously harmed. Carcasses were donated to nearby Native Americans. During the first winter reduction, 2,598 animals were killed outside Yellowstone, and 667 were destroyed within. For similar ecological reasons, workers in Rocky Mountain and Glacier sporadically hunted elk. The last "reduction" in Yellowstone was in 1967.

- With the blessing of the National Park Service's first director, Yosemite established a zoo—complete with cougars—so that tourists might see the more popular animals. From 1920 to 1933, a herd of tule elk from the San Joaquin Valley was penned in a twenty-eight-acre meadow in Yosemite Valley "for the pleasure and education of the visitors." Yellowstone set up a zoo with bison, bears, coyotes, and a badger in 1925.

- Reacting to the devastating effects that feral (once domestic) burros were having on the landscape, Grand Canyon rangers began eradicating the pack-animals-gone-wild in 1924; by 1969 they had killed 2,888 of the creatures.

- For three days in December 1924, in an effort to avert mass starvation of at least thirty thousand deer on the Grand Canyon's isolated North Rim, 150 men tried to drive some eight thousand

National Park Service hydrologist Larry Martin collects scientific data on a research trip at the bottom of the Grand Canyon in 1993. BOB KRUMENAKER COLLECTION

emaciated animals down off the eight-thousand-foot plateau and across the Colorado River. The attempt was a total failure; deer easily doubled back between the cowboys. According to author Zane Grey, who was looking for book material as well as riding in the roundup, "The failure of the Grand Canyon deer drive might be laid to three causes—inadequate preparation, lack of enough drivers, and the total unexpected refusal of the deer to herd." The huge buildup of deer was the direct result of years of systematic removal of mountain lions from the area.

NOTE

I am deeply indebted to National Park Service Historian Richard W. Sellars and his 1997 book, *Preserving Nature in the National Parks: A History,* for much of the information in this section.

Chapter 8
WOMEN RANGERS

At peak summer season, there are almost twenty-six thousand permanent and seasonal employees in the National Park Service, and approximately ninety-two hundred of them are women. From the beginning of the park system, women were there, making an indelible mark. They now serve alongside men as rangers, truck drivers, interpreters, personnel officers, scientists, historians, administrators, laborers, managers, architects, mule wranglers, planners, curators, clerks, and dispatchers.

Women have left an extraordinary legacy through their contributions to the national parks as early travelers and explorers, conservationists and advocates, concessionaires and wives, and, more recently, as "real" National Park Service rangers and employees. Not only were they among the first to climb peaks, roam the wilderness, and float rivers, but women also endured a harsh frontier life, raised the first children born in parks, ran primitive log hostelries and fed the tourists, and served as early nature guides.

Women erected monuments to men of the Union and the Confederacy who never returned from Gettysburg, Shiloh, and Vicksburg, and much later helped ensure we would never forget that as a nation we interned our Japanese-American neighbors during World War II. They worked to protect the Joshua trees of California's desert as well as the lush redwood forests to the north, home of the world's tallest trees. Women made sure that the principal story of Virginia's first settlement at Jamestown was told, and as early as 1882, recognized the worth of the ancient cliff dwellings at Mesa Verde. They saved the rain forests of the Olympic Peninsula from the sawyers, and it was a woman

(Marjory Stoneman Douglas) whose writing and advocacy directly led to the protection of the Everglades, the last remnant of this country's subtropical wilderness.

Ironically, for reasons now viewed as sexist and irrational, until far into the twentieth century women had extremely limited opportunities to join the ranger ranks of the National Park Service. A 1965 Federal Civil Service recruitment flyer noted that: "Park ranger positions are restricted to men, due to the rugged, and sometimes hazardous nature of the duties."

EXPLORERS AND TRAVELERS

Women were responsible for a number of impressive explorations and physical feats in the national parks.

Three women wearing long skirts, enthusiastic but somewhat drained by their long trip, rode sidesaddle into Yosemite Valley in 1856. Only five years after the Mariposa Battalion had driven the local Indians from the area and eight years before the valley was set aside as a park by Congress, Madame Gautier, Jean Frances Neal, and "Mrs. Thompson" were the first Euro-American women to witness the grandeur that is Yosemite.

In 1864, Helen Brodt became the first woman to climb Mount Lassen; the party accompanying her discovered a lake and named it for her. Botanist Ellen Powell Thompson, sister of Major John Wesley Powell, joined her brother in floating the Colorado River on his second expedition in 1871, the same year that Addie Alexander of St. Louis summited the highest point in what would become Rocky Mountain National Park. This ascent of Longs Peak was one of the earliest of a big mountain by a woman in the nineteenth century.

Historians believe that Emma Stone of Bozeman, Montana, traveling with her husband and two sons in July 1872, was the first non-Indian woman to visit Yellowstone, four months after it became the world's only national park. That same year in Hawaii, Isabella Bird scrambled to the rim of fourteen-thousand-foot Mauna Loa after having descended to the lake of molten lava at the bottom of nearby Halemaumau Crater.

In 1878, four women from the San Joaquin Valley spent a month camping and riding before topping California's Mt. Whitney, the highest peak in the

United States. One of those women had been lame since childhood, but teacher Anna Mills believed her "surplus of determination" made up for any of her physical defects.

Eliza Scidmore, the only female board member of the National Geographic Society, was a ship passenger on the *Idaho* in 1883 as it entered Glacier Bay carrying the first visitors to this mountainous area of southeast Alaska; Scidmore Bay is named for her. Seven years later, at 4:30 P.M. on August 10, 1890, twenty-year-old Fay Fuller, wearing a long skirt, became the first woman to look down from the top of Washington's ice-covered 14,410-foot-high Mount Rainier, fifth highest point in the United States. (Not until the final days of suffrage did women travel in long pants without shocking their male climbing partners.)

GUIDES AND RANGERS

Though they couldn't be employed as official "rangers," many women found work in the national parks quite early on. For one month in 1914, Ester Cleveland Brazell worked as a guide at South Dakota's Wind Cave. She is very likely the first woman on the federal rolls in a ranger-like position in a park. Married to the superintendent (the only permanent employee in the park), she was probably appointed in late summer by her husband to assist two or three other guides who conducted the fifty cent, twice-daily, three-hour cave trips.

Two years later, Elizabeth and Esther Burnell visited the newly established Rocky Mountain National Park. Elizabeth was a teacher of college mathematics with an advanced degree from the University of Michigan. Having passed the "nature teacher" test, the sisters were licensed by the park as guides in the summer of 1917. Although not actually employed by the government, they were the first women officially designated as naturalists by the National Park Service. Elizabeth directed the Enos Mills' Trail School for twelve summers and became the first woman guide on 14,255-foot-high Longs Peak.

In 1914, at the age of fourteen, Claire Marie Hodges rode a horse for four days to reach Yosemite; she began teaching there two years later. In the spring of 1918 she learned that Superintendent "Dusty" Lewis was looking for a woman to fill in as a ranger because many male employees had been sent off to war; her application was forwarded to Washington and quickly accepted. Accordingly, she became the second woman park ranger in the National Park

Seen here in 1918, Yosemite's Temporary Ranger Claire Marie Hodges was authorized to wear a sidearm but seldom did. Only eighteen years of age in this photo, she was the Service's second woman to work in a ranger position. NATIONAL PARK SERVICE, HARPERS FERRY CENTER ARCHIVES

Service. Reporting to the chief ranger, Hodges often patrolled both the valley and more remote areas of the park on horseback. She wore the traditional ranger's Stetson hat, but her divided skirt and a ranger badge pinned to her middy blouse distinguished her from her male co-workers. Although authorized to carry a gun, she seldom did.

Only six weeks after Hodges, Helene Wilson was hired at Mount Rainier. Like her Yosemite counterpart, she filled in for men who were entering military service that year. Working at Nisqually, the park's main entrance, she recorded the engine number, license plate, and occupants' names and addresses for each car that entered. Ranger Wilson and a male coworker issued entry permits for more than eighteen thousand people that August. Three other women were employed in the national parks as seasonal rangers during the summer of 1918; they were posted at Glacier, Sequoia, and Yellowstone.

Newly married Isabel Bassett Wasson, who had just completed her master's degree in geology at Columbia, became Yellowstone's first female naturalist in

1920. She observed that her position was "ideal for teaching.... People were on vacation with the time to explore, observe, and grope for explanations of the natural wonders around them." Wasson spent just one summer working for the service (she became pregnant and joined her husband elsewhere), and was the first of only ten women to serve as rangers in Yellowstone for over the next forty years.

Marguerite Lindsley soon followed Wasson. Born and raised in Yellowstone, Marguerite was destined to be a Yellowstone ranger. The daughter of the park's chief clerk (who later served as acting superintendent for three years), Lindsley lived in the park during both the military and civilian administrations. She recalled the pageantry of the cavalry: "bugle calls, sunrise and sunset guns, regimental bands, post flags at half mast for Decoration Day." An accomplished horsewoman, cross-country skier, and trans-continental motorcyclist, she possessed a broad knowledge of the natural history of the park and loved the wilderness. Hired seasonally in 1921 while still a college student, she enjoyed a ten-year career. In 1925, she became the agency's first permanent female ranger-naturalist.

In the summer of 1926, Yellowstone had five women working as rangers—two at entrance stations, one in the chief ranger's office, a naturalist at Camp Roosevelt, and Marguerite Lindsley (Arnold). Many male employees feared that the ranger image would become feminized given their perception of naturalists as effeminate. Yellowstone's Superintendent Horace Albright, however, recognized the merits of women and said of his male rangers, "There is not a member of the permanent force at the present time who could give a lecture if he had to—not even if his life depended on it." He was proud of his staff, but noted. "Of 31 permanent rangers not over half of them are good public contact men and several of these men we would not put in contact with the public at all. We keep them in outlying sections on fire patrol, and protection work."

In Yosemite, forty-year-old Enid Reeves Michael, wife of the local postmaster, began a two-decade-long career as a seasonal naturalist in 1921. Unlike her few contemporaries in other parks, she was never issued a badge or uniform. Each summer she led nature walks and maintained both a wildflower display and garden. In 1923 she, along with the head of the California Federation of Women's Clubs, pressured Director Stephen Mather to make her a permanent botanist for the park. Due to subtle internal politics as well as some local opposition, the attempt backfired, and Enid almost lost her job. She ended her employment in 1943 when the war forced drastic staffing cuts in the parks.

With a broad range of skills and talents, wives performed almost every function in the national parks. They worked without real authority, however, usually under the direction of their husbands. Many wives stationed with husbands in the System's remote archeological areas in the Southwest were formally designated "Honorary Custodian Without Pay" by Southwestern Monuments Superintendent "Boss" Pinkley. These couples—often the only staff in isolated parks such as Northern Arizona's Wupatki or Navajo National Monuments— spent much of their marriages in

Armed with an advanced degree in botany, Herma Albertson Baggley was the first woman the National Park Service selected to be a ranger-naturalist from the government's civil service employment register. She is shown here in Yellowstone in 1929.
NATIONAL PARK SERVICE, YELLOWSTONE NATIONAL PARK ARCHIVES

tents, Indian ruins, hogans, or just sleeping bags on the ground while living out of pickup trucks.

Between 1923 and 1928, working ranger wives were actually fairly compensated in Yosemite. The federal Classification Act of 1923 required that these women be paid equally for their seasonal work. For two years, Beatrice and Ed Freeland earned the same rate of pay for checking in cars at an entrance station. Working as a team, they operated their post from six in the morning until ten at night, seven days a week.

Rocky Mountain National Park hired Margaret Fuller Boos—its first ranger-naturalist—for the summers of 1928 and 1929, and put her in uniform like the men. When the superintendent wrote her about the job, he said he would "prefer a man for the work," even though she held a doctorate in geology.

He did appreciate her experience in public speaking and teaching, and recognized that she had "several hundred dollars' worth of lantern slides." As at most parks in that era, the slide collection was poor, so Boos's naturalist duties included taking photos for the government. She went on to establish the Department of Geology at the University of Denver.

While working for three summers as a chambermaid at Yellowstone's Old Faithful Lodge, Herma Albertson volunteered her free time as a nature guide. Beginning in 1926, she came to enjoy the respect of her peers and was eventually hired as a seasonal park naturalist in 1929. Two years later and armed with a new master's degree in botany from the University of Idaho, Herma became the first woman the National Park Service selected to be a ranger-naturalist from the government's civil service employment register. When she passed the junior park naturalist examination that year, Yellowstone offered her a permanent job. She demonstrated great promise in her new career, but resigned in December 1933, after marrying Chief Ranger George Baggley. After Herma, Yellowstone National Park hired just two more women as ranger-naturalists over the course of the next three decades.

In the Grand Canyon, Pauline Mead, a graduate student in botany at the University of Chicago, became the park's first woman ranger in 1929. Dressed in a male-styled uniform, she was encouraged to wear something more feminine than the traditional "flathat" or Stetson. She adopted a light-colored, soft-brimmed felt

Because there was no official policy from Washington, early women rangers wore whatever the superintendent or their own interests dictated. This coat was red and may have been worn by Yellowstone's Marguerite "Peg" Lindsley, the agency's first permanent female ranger-naturalist.
NATIONAL PARK SERVICE, HARPERS FERRY CENTER ARCHIVES

hat, similar to that worn by the female guides working for the local Fred Harvey Company. A good friend of the daughter of the service's first director, she married the park's assistant superintendent, Preston Patraw, in the spring of 1931. This ended her seasonal career.

Jobs began to open up for women in the museum field. Mesa Verde hired Caroline Thompson in the summer of 1932 as the park's first female museum assistant. An anthropology major at Bryn Mawr, she was the only woman among the dozen employees on the seasonal staff. In 1933, Betty Yelm, another anthropology student, read that the government was testing for

Ranger Anna Pigeon,
Mystery Writer Nevada Barr

Forty-something and independent, Anna Pigeon is a free-spirited, "wine-drinking, tough talking" National Park ranger—the fictitious heroine in the critically acclaimed Nevada Barr mystery series. Beginning in 1993 with *Track of the Cat*, Ranger Pigeon is entangled in at least one murder in every area in which she works. In this first book, she patrols the backcountry of the Guadalupe Mountains National Park of west Texas. When a coworker is seemingly clawed to death by a rogue mountain lion, Anna reluctantly gets involved.

Pigeon has "fought crime" underwater at Isle Royale and among Mesa Verde's Anasazi ruins. Taking emergency shelter from a raging forest fire she is battling in California, Pigeon discovers her partner has mysteriously died. As a park ranger in New Mexico, she is trapped in a cave hundreds of feet below ground, the victim of a landslide caused by a rescuer hiding a violent crime. She goes on to solve murders in Georgia's Cumberland Island, the Statue of Liberty, the Natchez Trace, Glacier, and Dry Tortugas. To date, Ranger Anna Pigeon has seen law enforcement duty in at least ten areas of the System.

Nevada Barr was both a seasonal and permanent park ranger before leaving to write full-time. Nevada—named not for the state in which she was born but rather for a character in one of her father's favorite books—first pursued a career in the theater and performed in several off-Broadway plays. She appeared in television commercials and industrial films before meeting her real-life park ranger husband and joining him in the Service. She began writing seriously in 1978. In 1993, Barr won the Agatha Award for Best First Mystery Novel and has been praised in national book reviews for "spectacular descriptions, psychological insight, and a refreshingly independent heroine."

Fort Jefferson, location for an Anna Pigeon mystery, took twenty years to build beginning in 1846. The largest all-masonry fortification in the western world, it is in Dry Tortugas National Park, halfway between Florida and Cuba. NATIONAL PARK SERVICE ARCHIVES

junior park archeologists; the announcement did not indicate that the jobs were "for men only." She was selected as a museum assistant on a permanent basis, although furloughed for seven months a year due to budget constraints (such breaks in service being common for both men and women at the time). At Arizona's Montezuma Castle, archeologist Sallie Pierce was hired for the winter of 1934 to classify recently excavated artifacts, but did not return to a similar paid career until after World War II.

Becoming a woman ranger was still nearly impossible, and by the mid-1930s, the hiring of women as permanent naturalists had ended. Because they believed that male naturalists would be labeled feminine and ridiculed by those more steeped in the Service's male traditions, some parks reportedly picked college football players to fill their seasonal naturalist positions.

During the 1940s and early '50s, there were a few "rangerettes" (a title that sounds insulting now) hired by the National Park Service, largely because of the effects of World War II. They worked mostly as guides and information-receptionists in areas like Glacier, Wind Cave, Morristown, and Edison.

In 1961, John F. Kennedy established the President's Commission on the Status of Women, naming Eleanor Roosevelt chair of the group. President Kennedy directed the Civil Service Commission to make the federal government the single largest employer of women and "a showcase ... of equality of opportunity." In the mid-1960s, women were routinely hired as naturalists, but it was not until the early 1970s that they began to be assigned more "rugged" duties such as law enforcement, search and rescue, animal control, and fire fighting.

Today, women occupy all levels of the organization, from field ranger to director. Such success has been hard earned; the National Park Service has come a long way since Ester Brazell served her brief stint in 1914. There are more female district and chief rangers than ever before, and women serve as superintendents of many parks, often in high-profile areas such as Glacier, Yosemite, Yellowstone, Great Smoky Mountains, and Everglades. At the national level, there have been at least three women regional directors and a chief and deputy chief of the United States Park Police. In 2001, Ms. Fran Mainella was confirmed by Congress as the sixteenth director of the National Park Service.

NOTE

I am deeply indebted to Polly Welts Kaufman and her 1996 book, *National Parks and the Woman's Voice*, for most of the information in this section.

Young minds absorb as Ranger Kym Elders speaks about Frederick Douglass, the nation's leading nineteenth-century African American spokesman.
NATIONAL PARK SERVICE, FREDERICK DOUGLASS NATIONAL HISTORIC SITE ARCHIVES

Photographed in 1962, Hawaii Volcanoes ranger Mitsuko T. Shikuma acknowledges the contribution that Stephen T. Mather made to the national parks. Plaques similar to this were purchased with private funds and dedicated in most parks during that era.
NATIONAL PARK SERVICE, HARPERS FERRY CENTER ARCHIVES

Chapter 9
GREATS OF THE GREEN AND GRAY
THE RANGER
HALL OF FAME

STEPHEN T. MATHER
(1867–1930)

The National Park Service's first director, Stephen Tyng Mather, was a self-made millionaire, who used a borax mining operation in California to develop great wealth. A strong supporter of the national park concept, Mather was challenged in 1915 by then Secretary of the Interior Franklin Lane to serve as his special assistant. In that role, Mather became a successful lobbyist for the parks, urging the creation of a special agency to manage them. He was named director of the new National Park Service in 1917 and served in the position until 1929.

Combining a preservation ethic with marketing foresight, Mather was the perfect person to lead the fledgling agency. He designed the organizational framework still largely used by the Park Service, and used his numerous civic, fraternal, and business affiliations to advance his vision for the national parks. He saw the need for interpretation programs, for road and other infrastructure development, and for improved concession facilities to accommodate an increasing number of visitors, often spending his own funds to improve the

> In August 1926, Custodian Neil Erickson of Arizona's Walnut Canyon National Monument was awarded a Special Congressional Medal of Honor "for valorous service in the United States Army" from 1879 to 1886, "during which time he took part as scout in the campaign against Geronimo, the Apache chieftain."

Beginning in 1919 and for ten years, Horace M. Albright was both Superintendent of Yellowstone National Park as well as the agency's Assistant Director for Field Operations. Notice the two stars on his right wrist, signifying ten years of service. This photo was taken in Yellowstone in 1926. NATIONAL PARK SERVICE, YELLOWSTONE NATIONAL PARK ARCHIVES

parks when federal support was unavailable. His greatest contribution, however, was in recognizing the need to develop support of national parks by both the "grass roots" public as well as the "movers and shakers" of the day, and then in capitalizing on this interest to further the goals of the service. The many bronze plaques dedicated in his honor around the National Park System summarize Stephen Tyng Mather's lifelong contribution:

> He laid the foundation of the National Park Service, defining and establishing the policies under which its areas shall be developed and conserved, unimpaired for future generations. There will never come an end to the good he has done.

HORACE M. ALBRIGHT
(1890 – 1987)

Horace Marden Albright was a twenty-three-year-old recent graduate of the University of California at Berkeley when he arrived in Washington on May 31, 1913, to work for the newly appointed Secretary of the Interior. Attending Georgetown University School of Law at night, Albright was a staff assistant for Secretary Franklin Lane, with a variety of administrative charges, some dealing with parks. Late in 1914 Albright met Mather for the first time; a friendship quickly blossomed, and Albright became Mather's trusted assistant. The men formed a lifelong bond of respect and mutual regard.

Horace Albright worked unsparingly for passage of the National Park Service Act of 1916, and when its new director, Stephen Mather, suffered a nervous breakdown the next year, filled in as the agency's acting director. For the next dozen years, Albright took on many of the director's professional burdens and functioned as the man "behind the scenes." Beginning in 1919 and for the next ten years, Albright was the Superintendent of Yellowstone National Park while serving simultaneously as Assistant Director for Field Operations. When his good friend and chief retired in January 1929, Albright became the service's second director. He served as director of the National Park Service until 1933, when he voluntarily resigned to enter private business. Before his death in 1987 at the age of ninety-six, he received a host of honors and awards for his abundant contributions to America's national park heritage.

Greats of the
Green and Gray

DR. HAROLD C. BRYANT
(1886 – 1968)

Dr. Harold Bryant was largely responsible for developing the first education programs in the national parks; his work laid the foundation for interpretive programs that are offered by almost all land management agencies today. While vacationing at Lake Tahoe in 1919, Director Stephen Mather attended one of Bryant's weekly nature programs at a local lodge and was so impressed that he persuaded the zoologist from the University of California at Berkeley to present similar programs the next summer in Yosemite.

Bryant and his coworker Dr. Loye Holmes Miller (both men working without pay) led nature field trips and offered evening campfire programs in the park for three summers. In 1923 Bryant was appointed a seasonal ranger, and two years later became the first director of the Yosemite School of Field Natural History—a new institution for training naturalists. Hundreds of seasonal and permanent ranger-naturalists profited from this training until the school was discontinued in 1953.

Dr. Bryant also served as the educational director of the California Fish and Game Commission until 1930, when he assumed a permanent position with the National Park Service as assistant director of the Branch of Research and Education, a job he held for eight years. Dr. Bryant helped establish both Olympic and Kings Canyon National Parks, and served as the superintendent of Grand Canyon National Park from 1941 until 1954.

FRANK "BOSS" PINKLEY
(1881 – 1940)

"Boss" Pinkley spent his thirty-nine-year parks career preserving the vanishing cultural treasures of the Southwest. A little more than a year after moving to Phoenix in 1900 to convalesce from tuberculosis, the twenty-year-old Pinkley took work as the government's caretaker at nearby Casa Grande Ruin Reservation. Living in a tent and making do with very little, Pinkley became captivated by these exceptional prehistoric ruins. He dedicated himself to protecting and learning about them and spent the next seventeen years unraveling their mystery. When the ruins were made a part of the National Park System in 1918, Pinkley became custodian at the new monument (a job similar to that of superintendent in a national park), as well as at several other areas in Arizona.

Frank Pinkley at Casa Grande National Monument in 1934. Outspoken but with a great sense of humor, the "Boss" was responsible for the oversight of twenty-seven national monuments in four states when he died "with his boots on" of a heart attack on February 14, 1940. WESTERN ARCHEOLOGICAL CENTER ARCHIVES

Ansel Hall stands beside the cornerstone for the new Yosemite Museum, begun in 1924. Serving as a naturalist for the park from 1920 to 1923, he was largely responsible for raising private funds for this state-of-the-art facility.

Despite ever-increasing visitation from a curious and interested public, Pinkley's small monuments and related areas received little funding; they were continually overshadowed by the more famous, "big-name" parks. Pinkley often traveled at his own expense or went without salary to provide much-needed repairs for the areas in his care, and he relied upon his great sense of humor to survive often difficult times. A vocal critic of bureaucracy but a grand student of human nature, Pinkley was respected for his forceful but fatherly management style. On February 14, 1940, after delivering the keynote address at the first school of Instruction for Custodians of the Southwestern Monuments (a twenty-year-old dream of his), he sat down and suffered a fatal heart seizure. At the time of his death "Boss" Pinkley was responsible for oversight of twenty-seven national monuments in four states.

> Due to a heroic act during a rescue in 1929, Mt. Rainier's temporary ranger Charlie Browne became the first of only two people to ever receive a presidential appointment as a permanent park ranger. Mt. Rainier's Bill Butler became the second in 1936, also for a daring rescue effort on the 14,410-foot-high peak.

ANSEL HALL
(1894 – 1962)

Ansel Hall was the National Park Service's first chief naturalist and chief forester (a combined responsibility early in the two programs). Born in Oakland, he graduated from the University of California in 1917 with a degree in forestry. He began his career in Sequoia as a ranger but soon saw service in France during World War I. Hall, with a genuine love of both nature and children and gifted instinctively as a teacher, rose rapidly through the ranks of the recently created agency. After being park naturalist in Yosemite from 1920 to 1923, Ansel Hall served for the next fourteen years as the Service's chief naturalist, chief forester, and then finally head of its newly formed Field Division.

According to one biographical sketch, Hall "was a rare combination of romantic idealist and practical businessman." With this talent, he personally raised much of the private funds with which the Yosemite National Park museum was built. He also developed the park's museum association, the first of the service's many current cooperating associations. He was an intuitive manager, able to put the "right person in the right job." Hall was charming and persuasive and a key leader in the agency in the 1930s era of federal public works and related welfare programs. He was a mentor to photographer Ansel Adams,

Greats of the
Green and Gray

raised significant money for creation of the regional parks in the Bay Area, and organized Eagle Scout trips to Costa Rica. Ansel Hall left the National Park Service in 1938 to run the concession operations in Mesa Verde.

George Wright, chief of the agency's Wildlife Division, circa 1935.
NATIONAL PARK SERVICE, HARPERS FERRY CENTER ARCHIVES

GEORGE M. WRIGHT
(1904–1936)

George Melendez Wright is considered the "father" of scientific biological research (including wildlife management) in the National Park Service. Although he worked just nine years with the agency, Wright indelibly left his mark, not only within the service but also within the national resource conservation community. A graduate in forestry from the University of California at Berkeley, he began his parks career as an assistant park naturalist in Yosemite in 1927. At the time neither the service nor other land management agencies had science or wildlife programs devoted to field research, and there were no employees working as park resource managers or game biologists.

Wright proposed and then spearheaded the first servicewide wildlife survey in 1929, personally funding the project for several years. The initiative prompted parks throughout the system to study the status of their larger animals and identify associated management concerns. Four years later, these findings were published in the landmark document, *Fauna of the National Parks of the United States, a Preliminary Survey of Faunal Relations in National Parks.* Wright's next position was to oversee the research efforts of the Park Service's newly established Wildlife Division, but he was never to accomplish all he had planned. In 1936, Wright was killed in a car wreck in New Mexico while on agency business. To honor his many contributions, the George Wright Society was founded in 1980, and the organization has become a national clearinghouse for those engaged in scientific activities within the world's parks and protected areas.

FRANK KOWSKI (1910–1975)

Frank Kowski, known for his depth of knowledge about the art of rangering, was esteemed (and sometimes idolized) by young rangers over several generations. Beginning as a backcountry ranger in Yellowstone in 1937, he became a student of the history and lore that were essential to any ranger's success. His interest in, and love for, the mission of the National Park Service and the traditions and work of the ranger made him the perfect pick to be the agency's first director of training (a job he took in 1951).

Over nearly two decades Kowski was a mentor to thousands. Unbending in his vision and dedication, he established one of the federal government's earliest facilities for training. First located in Yosemite in 1957 and moved to the Grand Canyon in 1962, "Kowski Kollege" (a name he hated) is still in operation, helping shape the careers of employees of the service.

> Frederick Sisneros, working until the day he died in 1988, four days short of his ninety-fourth birthday, was the oldest active ranger in the Service. In 1899, at the age of five, his father instructed him to "Look after the ruins, to run and tell him or [his] mother if I saw anyone disturbing this historic treasure." For eighty-nine years, Sisneros guarded San Gregorio de Abo Mission, now part of New Mexico's Salinas National Monument.

Kowski served as Superintendent of Sequoia-Kings Canyon National Parks for a year in 1966, then became regional director for several dozen parks and monuments in the Southwest for the next seven years. Despite his "rough and tumble" exterior (including an omnipresent cigar), Frank Kowski had a heart as big as the parks he loved and he is fondly remembered still as "Mr. Training" within the National Park Service.

GEORGE B. HARTZOG (1920–)

George Hartzog began his career, not in the national parks, but as a Methodist preacher in South Carolina at age seventeen. He studied law at night and was admitted to the state's bar when he was just twenty-two. Following military service as a captain in the army during World War II, Hartzog took a job as an attorney for the National Park Service in 1945. Over the next twenty-eight years he served in a variety of Park Service positions, from legal counsel to superintendent. In January 1964 he became the agency's seventh director. During his nine-year tenure as chief, sixty-nine new areas were added to the park system.

George Hartzog, a natural leader, was very politically astute. He worked closely with Congress, cooperating when appropriate, and taking aggressively

Greats of the
Green and Gray

defensive positions on behalf of his agency at other times. He began his administration by formally organizing the nearly 250 areas within the System into three categories: natural, historical, or recreational. Hartzog also is credited with orchestrating passage of the act that set aside eighty million acres of Alaska wildlands as parks, refuges, and wilderness. Faced with considerable civil and social upheaval during his directorship, Hartzog worked to ensure that his agency reflected the make-up of the general population through notable appointments of women and minorities, and also initiated innovative environmental and educational programs.

RUSSELL E. DICKENSON
(1922–)

In his stellar thirty-eight-year National Park Service career, Russ Dickenson distinguished himself by becoming the first ranger to rise through the ranks from entry-level ranger to the lofty heights of the directorship. After graduating from Northern Arizona University and serving in the Marine Corps in World War II, Dickenson began as a "buck" ranger at the Grand Canyon in 1946. His subsequent ranger assignments took him to Chiricahua National Monument, and Big Bend, Glacier, and Zion National Parks. He was assigned to a number of important posts, including chief ranger at Grand Teton National Park.

During the next two decades, he served as regional director of two different regions—one on each coast—and was the agency's number two official under two directors. Enjoying the respect of his colleagues throughout all levels of the Service, Russ Dickenson was appointed director (the agency's eleventh) in May 1980, where he continued until March 1985. Unlike previous directors who expanded the park system only to find that they lacked much-needed fiscal support and appropriations, Dickenson elected to work to improve those park areas already established.

A recipient of numerous well-deserved awards and honors, perhaps Dickenson's single greatest achievement for the agency was formulating the Service's Park and Restoration Improvement Program, which infused the parks with more than a billion dollars over a five-year period to stabilize and upgrade existing resources, infrastructure, and facilities. Russell E. Dickenson, however, would like nothing more than to be remembered as just a "field ranger—serving the park visitor and protecting the parks."

Ranger Russ Dickenson at the Grand Canyon in 1948. Russ was the first ranger to work his way up the ranks to become Director of the National Park Service. RUSSELL DICKENSON COLLECTION

Harry Yount Award: Protection

"Rocky Mountain Harry" Yount is generally credited as the first national park ranger. He was a frontiersman, Civil War veteran, guide, professional hunter, and bullwhacker. On June 21, 1880, he was appointed Gamekeeper in Yellowstone National Park by the Secretary of the Interior, and it was his primary duty to keep the park's wildlife from being slaughtered by commercial hunters.

The Harry Yount Award, sponsored by the National Park Foundation, is bestowed annually on that person who exemplifies the best of the ranger tradition. The first Yount Award was given at a regional level to Judith Knuth Folts of Cuyahoga Valley National Recreation Area in 1992, and it became a national honor in 1994. The honoree is selected from among the service's regional Yount recipients. On occasion the award—including a nearly life-sized bust of Yount created by Susanne Vertel—has been presented by the President of the United States at the White House.

Ranger Jim Brady receives the Harry Yount Lifetime Achievement Award from President Clinton in the Oval Office in April 1997. Jim's successful career would not have been possible without the unfailing efforts of his wife Gwen. GWEN BRADY COLLECTION

National Harry Yount Award Recipients

1994	Joe Fowler, Lake Clark National Park
1995	Jim Hannah, Wrangell-St. Elias National Park
1996	Tommie Lee, Glen Canyon National Recreation Area
1998	Mike Anderson, Cape Hatteras National Seashore
1999	Dale Antonich, Lake Mead National Recreation Area
2000	Stuart Schneider, Great Sand Dunes National Monument
2001	Hunter Sharp, Wrangell-St. Elias National Park
2002	Wayne Valentine, Delaware Water Gap National Recreation Area

Harry Yount Lifetime Achievement Award

1994	Rick Gale, Deputy Chief Park Ranger: Fire, Aviation, Emergency Management
1994	Jack Davis, Associate Director (retired)
1997	Jim Brady, Superintendent, Glacier Bay National Park
2001	Butch Farabee, Assistant Superintendent, Glacier National Park (retired)

Freeman Tilden Award: Interpretation

Though he died at age ninety-three in 1980, Freeman Tilden is still both a hero and an admired figure to park rangers. A noted novelist and playwright earlier in his career, Tilden later wrote prodigiously about national parks, although he considered himself an amateur since he did not come up through the ranks. He "gave form and substance" to the art of interpretation with his monumental 1957 publication, *Interpreting Our Heritage*, which challenged generations of interpreters to provide meaning, relevance, and provocation for park visitors. Freeman Tilden is universally regarded as the "soul" of interpretation. An interpreter from each region is nominated each year for the Freeman Tilden Award, given jointly by the National Park Service and National Parks and Conservation Association. The winner is the park ranger who best demonstrates all the traits that Tilden valued in interpretation.

Despite having died in 1980, Freeman Tilden is still a very powerful influence on park rangers. BOB BINNEWEIS COLLECTION

Freeman Tilden Award Recipients

1982	Victor Jackson, Zion National Park
1983	Bruce Craig, Channel Islands National Park
1984	Sandra Dayhoff, Everglades National Park
1985	Walter McDowney, National Capital Parks-East
1986	Phillip Evans, Fort Raleigh National Historic Site
1987	Carol Spears, Cuyahoga Valley National Recreation Area
1988	Sylvia Flowers, Ocmulgee National Monument
1989	James Small, Andersonville National Historic Site
1990	Maureen Loughlin, Everglades National Park
1991	Wilson Hunter, Canyon de Chelly National Monument
1992	David Kronk, Everglades National Park
1993	Mark Wagner, Katmai National Park
1994	Kim Valentino, Northwest Alaska Areas
1995	Ray Morris, Fort Frederica National Monument
1996	Joseph Onofrey, Gettysburg National Military Park
1997	Chuck Arning, Blackstone River Valley National Heritage Corridor
1998	Sally Griffin, Catoctin Mountain Park
1999	Robert Woody, Cape Hatteras National Seashore
2000	Lana Henry, George Washington Carver National Monument
2001	Phil Zichterman, Curecanti National Recreation Area
2002	Melissa English-Rias, Martin Luther King Jr. National Historic Site

Stephen T. Mather Award: Park Resources Protection

The Stephen T. Mather Award, sponsored by the National Parks Conservation Association and named for the first director of the National Park Service, is conferred annually on a service employee who has exhibited exemplary and distinguished performance in park protection and enhancement through demonstrated initiative and resourcefulness in promoting resource protection. These people have taken direct action (where others may have hesitated) to reinforce good park stewardship and values, often doing so despite significant controversy and external pressures.

Stephen T. Mather Award Recipients

1984   William B. Jewell, Army
        Corps of Engineers for Big Thicket
        National Preserve

1985   Bob Haraden, Superintendent, Glacier National Park

1986   Jack Morehead, Superintendent, Everglades
        National Park

1987   Howard Chapman, Director,
        Western Region

1988   Norm Bishop,
        Yellowstone National Park Center
        for Resources

1989   Bob Barbee, Superintendent,
        Yellowstone National Park

1990   Boyd Evison, Director, Alaska Region

1991   Chris Shaver, Chief of Policy,
        Planning and Permits, Air Quality Division

1992   Bill Wade, Superintendent,
        Shenandoah National Park

1993   William Reilly, Administrator,
        Environmental Protection Agency

1994   Frank Buono, Instructor,
        Horace M. Albright Training Center

1995   Dan Kimball, Chief, Water Resources Division

1996   Riley Hoggard, Resources Management Specialist,
        Gulf Islands National Seashore

1997   Ernest Quintana, Superintendent,
        Joshua Tree National Park

1998   Dennis R. Davis, Superintendent,
        Cumberland Islands National Seashore

1999   "Costa" J. Dillon, Superintendent,
        Fire Island National Seashore

2000   John Donahue, Superintendent,
        Big Cypress National Preserve

2001   Stephen Martin, Superintendent,
        Denali National Park

2002   James Renfro, Air Resources Specialist,
        Great Smoky Mountains National Park

Chapter 10
RANGER DANGER

Working as a ranger in the national parks involves considerable risk, particularly due to the inherently dangerous nature of such duties as law enforcement, search and rescue, fire fighting, and backcountry and wilderness patrol. Though records are not complete, there have been numerous injuries to rangers since 1872, and at least fifty-two of them have died in the line of duty. While seventeen of those ranger fatalities have occurred since 1990, the job of park ranger is generally safer than law enforcement positions in urban and more heavily populated areas.

Rangers have died in many different ways. Since 1921, at least nineteen rangers have died accidentally by drowning, avalanche, falls, or exposure. Naturalist Glen Sturdevant, who was never found, apparently drowned in the Colorado River while studying the geology of the Grand Canyon in 1929. Assistant Chief Ranger Chuck Scarborough was knocked from his horse and crushed by a huge rockslide while on a Yosemite backcountry patrol in 1954.

Seventeen rangers have been killed while in a vehicle or aircraft, often while responding to an emergency or while engaged in search and rescues. Grand Canyon Seasonal Ranger Bill Hall died when his patrol car crashed en route to a serious motor vehicle accident on the park's North Rim in 1979. While searching for an elderly hiker in 1997, Seasonal Ranger Taryn Hoover and two rescue volunteers were fatally injured when the helicopter carrying them crashed on takeoff in the Olympic National Park backcountry.

Since 1927, when James Cary was slain by bootleggers at Hot Springs National Park, eight rangers have been murdered while on routine patrol or responding to a crime in progress. Seven of them were shot, including twenty-seven-year-old Kris Eggle, who was ambushed in a drug-related incident

James Cary, a ranger at Hot Springs National Park and the first one to be shot and killed, is believed to have been murdered by bootleggers. He died on March 12, 1927, at age 31.
NATIONAL PARK SERVICE, HOT SPRINGS NATIONAL PARK ARCHIVES

on August 9, 2002, in southern Arizona's isolated Organ Pipe Cactus National Monument. In 1973, Ranger Ken Patrick, a former highway patrolman, stopped three men, unaware that they were poachers, on a side road in California's Point Reyes National Seashore. An arrow from a crossbow ended his life that dark night. While chatting with visitors at Casa Grande National Monument, a young naturalist was struck and killed by a .22-caliber bullet in November 1974; the mysterious murder was never explained or solved.

Six rangers have died from heart attacks and two others simply vanished while on duty. Chiricahua National Monument's Paul Fugate left the park's visitor center for a late-afternoon hike and disappeared in 1980. His fate and whereabouts are unknown. Seasonal Ranger Randy Morgensen, an expert mountaineer with over thirty years on the job, went missing in the Kings Canyon backcountry in the summer of 1996. His body was found on July 15, 2001, in a remote location of the park, where he had apparently fallen and suffered a serious injury.

RANGERS AND EMERGENCY RESPONSE

In 2001—the last year that complete records were available—rangers and other employees of the National Park Service faced a daunting emergency workload. Most of these incidents took place within park areas, but employees did (and routinely do) respond to many crises outside their normal jurisdiction. The following are the 2001 statistics:

Silent in death, almost 1,000 feet below and at the edge of the molten fluid lay the 17-year-old girl and the jealous young man who had shot her. With Margaret locked in his arms he had hurled himself off the cliff and into the live volcano on June 2, 1932.
COURTESY OF *THE HAWAII PRESS*

John Fonda took this photo of the snowplane that delivered them to the trail, only hours before he and fellow ranger Gale Wilcox died of hypothermia while on a backcountry patrol in Grand Teton National Park in March 1960.

JOHN FONDA PHOTO, DOUG MCLAREN COLLECTION

For many decades the National Park Service has been the leader in search and rescue (SAR). This is the manual for the country's first SAR school.

DOUG MCLAREN COLLECTION

Fatalities

Traumatic (falls, drownings, etc.)	141
Nontraumatic (cardiac, "natural," etc.)	86

Medical Cases (EMS)

Advanced Cardiac Life Support	307
Advanced Life Support	1,884
Basic Life Support	2,281
Minor Medical	7,201

Search and Rescues (SAR).

Incidents/Missions	3,619
Individuals (lost, trapped, or involved)	4,407
Saves (would not have survived otherwise)	1,367

One of two climbing rescue caches located in Rocky Mountain National Park in 1940.
NATIONAL PARK SERVICE, ROCKY MOUNTAIN NATIONAL PARK ARCHIVES

Criminal Offenses

Part I Crimes (homicide, rape, robbery, burglary, etc.)	4,147
Part II Crimes (alcohol, disorderly, theft, vandalism, etc.)	50,894
Traffic Cases	54,336
Part I Crimes, Cleared by Arrest	592
Part II Crimes, Cleared by Arrest (some are released after a citation but are considered arrests)	27,555
Citations Issued (traffic other than Driving While Intoxicated)	54,336

Physical Assaults on Rangers

In 2001 (including one killed)	31

Fires

Wildland (for 192,881 acres)	640
Prescribed (for 132,655 acres)	319
Mutual Aid (times to adjoining agencies)	288
Support (other fires around country)	1,157
Structural (in 30 different areas)	92

Each park has one or more levels of jurisdiction: exclusive, concurrent, and proprietary. In exclusive only federal laws apply, in concurrent rangers enforce both state and federal, and in proprietary they enforce only state laws.
NATIONAL PARK SERVICE, ROCKY MOUNTAIN NATIONAL PARK ARCHIVES

CAN RANGERS MAKE ARRESTS?

Not all rangers have the power or responsibility to enforce the laws in the national parks. To make arrests, a ranger must be sufficiently trained so that he or she has earned the necessary qualification known as a "law enforcement commission." Nearly 1,540 permanent and almost 500 (2002) seasonal rangers possess law enforcement commissions. These rangers make arrests as well and issue violation notices for a wide range of offenses. Rangers who enforce the law must meet very strict training and fitness requirements, similar to those required by most police agencies. At the same time, most law enforcement rangers have duties in other park

With 300,000,000 visitors in park areas annually, it is no surprise that rangers make 28,000 arrests (many are released by citation) each year. Shenandoah's Dana Sullivan, here in a 1998 training exercise, refreshes her police skills by handcuffing ranger Carol Leggat.
NATIONAL PARK SERVICE, SHENANDOAH NATIONAL PARK ARCHIVES

Glacier ranger Don Dayton rescues the victim of a car wreck in 1958. He remembered his "flat hat" but forgot his life jacket. NATIONAL PARK SERVICE, GLACIER NATIONAL PARK ARCHIVES

areas, such as resource management, interpretation, fire, area management, and concessions.

Law enforcement rangers enforce many federal criminal laws. The laws embrace such common offenses as assault, theft, drugs, and vandalism, as well as less obvious violations related to health, safety, and the environment. Some of these same rangers can also enforce state criminal laws. They are, in effect, both federal as well as state law enforcement officers. In some areas with "exclusive jurisdiction," such as Denali, Sequoia, and Hawaii Volcano National Parks, rangers have broader legal authority and responsibility than do officers from every other agency and department in the country—certainly more than an FBI agent, a local sheriff's deputy, or a metropolitan policeman. In such parks, no other local law enforcement agencies have authority to act.

When a park covers areas in more than one state, the park rangers there often have federal enforcement authority in multiple states and are usually deputized in each state and county as peace officers. Some rangers, such as those in Yellowstone, are special United States Fish and Wildlife agents, or serve along the Canadian Border as customs officers (as do rangers in Glacier). There are some rangers in Yosemite and Yellowstone who perform as coroners.

Most authorized law enforcement rangers will carry weapons and related defensive equipment, although this is not always required. Unless a ranger is wearing a sidearm, there is nothing about the standard National Park Service uniform to indicate law enforcement authority.

A MILESTONE ARREST FOR RANGERS

In 1894, park officials were authorized to make arrests, but the federal government had not established penalties for criminal violations in the four national parks then existing. Law breakers might be physically ejected from a park, might have the tools of their crimes (such as guns) confiscated, or otherwise be harassed. But no one could be fined or imprisoned for poaching, grazing, timber harvesting, homesteading, mining, or related offenses in the national parks.

Things changed with the arrest of Edgar Howell for wanton killing of buffalo in Yellowstone National Park on March 13, 1894. Howell lived in Cooke City at Yellowstone's northeast corner and was seen suspiciously leaving the park one night early in March. For the next six days four soldiers, a scout, and

The author sits on a "gold mine." When one engine fell off a drug plane in December 1976, $200,000 worth of marijuana dropped into a backcountry lake in Yosemite. Due to weather, rugged terrain, and the isolated location, it took six months to "wrap" this SAR mission up.
AUTHOR'S COLLECTION

the park's photographer followed Howell's ski tracks. On the morning of March 13, two of the searchers discovered a small camp with six buffalo scalps and skulls. Howell's trail faded, but a scout named Burgess and an Army sergeant persisted and found a fresh track leading to a second lodge. Several shots were heard, and then the men encountered Howell.

> He [Burgess] performed an act of bravery that deserves especial mention and recognition. The poacher was undoubtedly armed with a repeating rifle; it was equally certain that he was a desperate character & would resist arrest even to the point of taking life. The only arms Burgess and the Sergeant carried was a single Army revolver. Notwithstanding the serious risk, they boldly started over the 400 yards of open valley. The poacher was so occupied in skinning his buffalo that he did not see Burgess until he was within 15 or 20 feet of him. He then started for his rifle, but on order from Burgess stopped and surrendered. Near him, were the bodies of 5 buffalo, freshly killed.

The confiscated heads of the dozen slaughtered bison were preserved as grisly trophies for display to select government officials. Because few wild buffalo remained in the United States (less than three hundred), Howell's crime was considered particularly egregious. Yellowstone's Acting Superintendent Anderson recommended that it "be made the occasion for a direct appeal to Congress for the passage of an act making it an offense" and that the punishment "should be graded between a small fine only and a long term of imprisonment."

Fortuitously, influential *Forest and Stream* reporter Emerson Hough and photographer F. J. Haynes were in the park at the time on another assignment. Outraged by the slaughter, they produced thirteen different articles about the incident that gained the attention of concerned citizens around the country. One of them was conservationist George Bird Grinnell, who pressured Congress to take steps to make sure that such wanton destruction was not repeated. Grinnell was persistent and the matter became the subject of national press attention. Federal legislators were inundated with petitions and letters from indignant constituents, and Iowa Congressman John F. Lacey was prompted to introduce a Yellowstone protection bill. After some thirty amendments, the bill was passed and then signed by President Grover Cleveland on May 7, 1894, less than two months after Edgar Howell had been arrested.

The Yellowstone Protection Act (also called the Lacey Act) represented the first time that park officials were given the authority to effectively enforce the laws of their jurisdictions. Among other penalties, fines and/or imprisonment could be imposed upon criminals, and the rule of law was finally established in the national parks.

DISASTERS AND OTHER MAJOR INCIDENTS

National Park Rangers, responsible for all aspects of visitor and resource protection in the parks, enjoy a well-earned, worldwide reputation for being competent. They have managed major oil spills, devastating forest fires, presidential visits, complicated searches, motorcycle rallies, remote plane wrecks, rock concerts, earthquakes, site dedications, unruly civil demonstrations, drug lab raids, manhunts, agency restructuring, and a host of other demanding situations.

Such challenges are managed using the Incident Command System (ICS)—a set of procedures used by emergency response agencies throughout the nation. The system was conceived in 1970 when firefighters from more than

The service's All-Risk Management Team, with some 350 people rotating in and out, spent more than three months in 1992 managing the catastrophic effects of Hurricane Andrew. This is the first time it was deployed in an emergency. It would not be the last.
NATIONAL PARK SERVICE, EVERGLADES NATIONAL PARK ARCHIVES

One of the very first two-way radios placed into a ranger patrol car in Rocky Mountain National Park in 1934. NATIONAL PARK SERVICE, ROCKY MOUNTAIN NATIONAL PARK ARCHIVES

Rangers first began using two-way radios in the summer of 1931 at Mt. Rainier. They could transmit between ten and twenty miles.

five hundred agencies, brought together to fight major fires in Southern California, recognized the need to develop better communication and cooperation. The ICS incorporates common terminology, standardized resources, structure, command, procedures, and decision-making. The National Park Service adopted the ICS in 1985, just after Queen Elizabeth and the royal party visited Yosemite.

Rangers deal with a wide variety of management issues. The security and "red carpet" treatment provided Queen Elizabeth II on her royal visit to Independence Hall and the Liberty Bell in 1976 consumed the Park Service for weeks.
NATIONAL PARK SERVICE, HARPERS FERRY CENTER ARCHIVES

Based on the magnitude and complexity of a situation, it is categorized by the ICS into one of three "types." Type I incidents are the most demanding—people and material are drawn from local, state, and national sources. High-profile newsmakers such as Hurricane Andrew require this level of reaction. Type II incidents are exacting enough to overwhelm the first responding agency; they are similar to Type I events, but without so large a size and impact. Type III occurrences are usually handled by in-house, "initial attack" resources.

Called "Mr. Rescue" by his peers, Mt. Rainier's Bill Butler (left) receives the Navy's highest civilian award for a search for thirty-two Marines who died in a plane crash in 1946. Butler received many similar citations during his long ranger career.
NATIONAL PARK SERVICE, MT. RAINIER NATIONAL PARK ARCHIVES

An example of a Type I incident was the lightning-ignited Shoshone Fire that grew into the many "Yellowstone Fires of 1988." At peak involvement, the fires necessitated the use of 9,500 firefighters, including 4,146 from the military, as well as 117 aircraft. Ultimately 25,000 people battled the blazes that burned 794,000 acres of the park. Park ranger Rick Gale was the overall ICS Area Commander, and fourteen of the country's eighteen Type I teams were deployed to Yellowstone during the struggle that lasted almost four months and cost $120 million.

In 1920, a "stout" Sequoia National Park visitor was forced to "starve" for three days by rangers in order for him to squeeze back through a hole in a cave in which he was stuck.

An emergency of another type was the environmental catastrophe that resulted when eleven million barrels of crude oil were spilled from a tanker (the *Exxon Valdez*) and defiled 1,244 miles of pristine Alaska shoreline. From March 1989, through the

Rangers respond to nearly 4,000 search and rescue missions annually. But for the combined efforts of both the Army and park staff, the climber in this 1977 accident on Mt. Rainier would have died. Note that only the rear of this Chinook helicopter is "parked" on the icy slope.
JOHN CONOBOY PHOTO

Ranger Jim Reilly administers medical aid to a stricken climber 2,000 feet up the face of Yosemite's El Capitan on June 2, 1981. JOHN DILL PHOTO

summer of 1991, nearly six hundred National Park Service employees responded to the ecological nightmare. When the job was complete, the park service organized the federal government's first Type I All-Risk Incident Management Team in 1991. Until that time, the country's Type I Teams had been oriented to fight fire, but the new "All-Risk" teams included people with skills to respond to a wide variety of situations.

The park service's Type I All-Risk Team was first deployed to Pearl Harbor in December 1991, for the emotion-laden fiftieth anniversary of the bombing

Moments after this dead climber was hoisted into the Navy helicopter at the base of Yosemite's El Capitan, one of its two engines quit and the million-dollar craft crashed and burned. No one was killed or injured in this June 16, 1975 mishap. DUTCH ACKART PHOTO

there. Since then, the agency's Type I and Type II teams have responded to dozens of disasters and other major events, managing incidents both inside and outside the National Park System.

RANGER FIREFIGHTERS

In its 1886 *Annual Report On Yellowstone National Park,* the United States Congress declared, "The most important duty of the superintendent . . . is to protect the forests from fire and axe." Management of fire has been a top priority in our parks since, and is increasingly being recognized for its positive, scientific value to the resource.

Before this badge was issued (1932 to 1946), fire guards used standard ranger badges when needed.
NATIONAL PARK SERVICE, HARPERS FERRY CENTER ARCHIVES

Fire, whether being fought or managed for the betterment of the land, is complicated and big business. During the decade 1990–1999, this country averaged over 106,000 wildfires each year; in 2000, there were 122,827, collectively burning an area larger than the

Not until the 1960s was there even minimum acceptance of fire as a positive factor in the ecosystem. Before that, all forest fires were "bad" and extinguished. This is probably a 1930s poster created by the Public Works Administration. WES KREIS COLLECTION

states of Connecticut and New Jersey combined. To suppress fires that one year cost taxpayers $1.36 billion. And this figure does not reflect the impact to an agency as people are called away from their normal jobs to respond to the emergency. The NPS, with almost thirty-eight hundred of its current employees trained and nationally certified ("Red Carded" as these credentials are known in the fire fighting community), is always well represented on these incidents. Most park rangers "eat smoke" during their career, some more than others. Two rangers illustrate this commitment to fire management.

Rangers who fought forest fires in the 1960s were often trained as "heli-jumpers." As the helicopter hovered over a clump of brush, they jumped to the ground. Despite the padding, the program was dangerous and short-lived. Rangers Jerry Chilton (left) and Ed Nelson are shown in full gear in 1966. ED NELSON COLLECTION

Steve Frye is Chief Ranger of Glacier National Park as well as an Incident Commander Type I on a National Interagency Incident Management Team. There are only sixteen Type I "overhead" teams in the United States. Each group, comprising men and women from different federal, state, and local agencies, may be deployed several times each year to the most complicated of national fire situations. When Steve's team is called out, fifty people go, all highly prepared to staff, supply, and combat a fire that may be hundreds of thousands of acres in size and last for months. Beginning with his first callout in 1965 and followed by thousands of hours of formal training since, Ranger Frye has been on over 250 fires. He oversaw one of 500,000 acres costing $146 million and another where thirty-four hundred firefighters fully occupied an entire county fairground for several months. Some park rangers have fought even more fires.

Rick Gale, a "Ranger's Ranger" and a recently retired National Type I Incident Commander, went on nearly three hundred fires during his forty-year career, occupying many of the eighty-six different positions possible on a large fire, from basic firefighter to area commander. In 1988, he oversaw the management of the nine fires that combined to burn 1,585,000 acres in the Greater Yellowstone Fire

Complex. The four-month-long national emergency required twenty-five thousand people and ultimately cost $125 million. Other than the fires of 1910 that joined to burn three million acres in Idaho and Montana, the Yellowstone conflagration was the largest in this country in the twentieth century.

The National Interagency Fire Center (NIFC) manages most of this country's wildfires. Based in Boise, Idaho, NIFC was started in 1965 and is now composed of seven land management agencies, including the National Park Service. It administers a broad, sophisticated system of oversight, support, and coordination, affecting everyone involved in wildfires as well as assisting on other large-scale emergencies such as hurricanes. Able to immediately supply ten thousand firefighters with basic equipment, it also provides over eighty different training courses for handling all aspects of fires and other events.

RANGER HEROES

On August 9, 1888, Army private John Coyle was patrolling the area near Yellowstone's Castle Geyser on foot, when he heard the panicked screams of a young woman. As it turns out, the adventuresome lass had climbed the cone of the geyser to look inside. When a wind shift left her enveloped in a cloud of steam, she became confused and disoriented. Unable to safely descend and fearful of falling into the geyser's yawning vent, she sounded her alarm. The quick-thinking Coyle dashed up the steep wall of the slippery, mineral-coated cone, wrapped his blue Army coat around the frightened woman, and led her to safety. In the process, the soldier seriously scalded his face. For this act of valor, John Coyle was awarded a silver medal from the United States Lifesaving Service, thus becoming the first person to be formally recognized for a rescue within a National Park Service area.

> The largest search in Park Service history began on June 14, 1969, when Dennis Martin disappeared in Great Smoky Mountains National Park; at least fourteen hundred people were involved at one time. The seven-year-old boy was never found.

A proposal for official recognition of acts of bravery by employees of the National Park Service was first put forward by an officer of the Zion National Park Lodge following a difficult rescue in that park in 1927: "Everyone is praising the work of the Rangers and Park Service men, including yours truly. They are so modest about it all. They risked their lives many times. . . . [S]uch work as this should not go unnoticed by the heads of the Department. There should be a medal of some sort for this kind of service."

Two years later, a six-person party was engulfed by a blizzard while ascending Mt. Rainier in July 1929. The party's chief guide, a veteran of forty-five climbs of the peak, described the storm as "the worst that I have ever experienced." For seven hours the group forced its way up the 14,410-foot peak, crawling the last one hundred yards due to gale-force winds. During the descent, the entire team lost its footing and slid one thousand feet down the ice-covered slope, then plunged into a seventy-five-foot-deep crevasse. Two members of the group died instantly and two were left unconscious.

Temporary ranger Charlie Browne, a tough and wiry climbing enthusiast of thirty-three, reacted quickly when he learned of the disaster far above. Braving the blinding storm alone while climbing over dangerous ice all night, Browne was able to engineer the rescue of the two seriously injured men and the body retrieval of the two dead. Browne received a promotion and modest pay increase for his work, and two days later, on July 24, 1929, he earned the first cita-

Three rangers in Sequoia, along with a local physician, were named in the Department of the Interior's first Unit Award for Valor. In 1951 they saved the life of a local fisherman through heroic effort and teamwork. Dick Boyer was one of these park rangers.
DICK BOYER COLLECTION

These seasonal rangers received the Service's Department of Interior Valor Award for a rescue in Rocky Mountain National Park in 1954. Left to right: Undersecretary of the Interior Chilson, Norm Nesbit, Bob Frauson, Jerry Hammond, and Frank Betts.
FRANK BETTS COLLECTION

tion for heroism ever issued by the Department of the Interior. In an unprecedented action, on September 27, President Herbert Hoover appointed Charles

Rocky Mountain National Park rangers Bob Haines (left) and Jim Randall ski in to the site of a winter mountaineering accident in 1969. Hundreds of search and rescue missions take place every winter in the national parks, requiring rangers to have ice, snow, and climbing skills. NATIONAL PARK SERVICE, ROCKY MOUNTAIN NATIONAL PARK ARCHIVES

In addition to receiving the Department of the Interior's first Valor Award, Charles Browne was appointed a permanent park ranger by President Herbert Hoover for a rescue on Mt. Rainier in 1929. At the time, Browne was earning $1,740 per year as a seasonal. NATIONAL ARCHIVES

E. Browne as a permanent national park ranger—a presidential act that has occurred only twice in the history of the National Park Service.

In 1955, the Department of the Interior created its own Valor Award. The criterion for the award is simple: an employee must "demonstrate unusual courage involving a high degree of personal risk in the face of danger." On May 30, 1956, Rocky Mountain National Park Rangers Frank Betts, Robert Frauson, Jerry Hammond, and Norman Nesbit, who had saved a seventeen-year-old novice climber who had fallen several feet onto a ledge, became the first in the Service to earn the Valor Award—in the form of a citation signed by the Secretary of the Interior accompanied by an engraved gold medal. Since then, this prestigious award has been granted to slightly fewer than two hundred courageous employees of the National Park Service.

Ranger Bill Nelson (with his horse Sheik) spent all night searching for the four-year-old girl who had wandered away from her campsite in Yosemite in 1932.
NATIONAL PARK SERVICE, YOSEMITE NATIONAL PARK RESEARCH LIBRARY

Mountain Troops

Still in existence today, the 10th Mountain Division has an incredible legacy.

On November 15, 1941, three weeks before the invasion of Pearl Harbor, the United States Army activated a new battle unit, the 87th Infantry Mountain Regiment. The War  Department recognized that Germany, Austria, Italy, and Russia had highly effective winter mountain troops. America had no fighters matching the skill of these European soldiers, so it quickly began training its own cadre of outdoor experts. The Army recruited men already proven capable of passing a night in the "woods" without dying of exposure or fright: lumberjacks, ski patrolmen, cowboys, and forest and park rangers.

For the next three years these soldiers skied, climbed, and trained on ice, snow, and rock. Determined crews worked with pack animals, improvised river crossings, and refined first aid and litter evacuation skills down tricky, steep cliffs. Outdoor gear that defined the standard for the next half century was developed and streamlined. New-style skis, boots, parkas, sleeping bags, stoves, cook kits, dehydrated foods, boot soles, ice axes, crampons, carabiners, and nylon ropes were either invented or refined.

Over the next several years the 10th Mountain Division evolved, distinguishing itself in Italy at the battles of Riva Ridge and Mt. Belvedere in 1945. Paying the supreme sacrifice, 990 of these soldiers never made it home. This elite unit is still a critical element of the United States Army today.

RANGERS, GO HOME!

President Jimmy Carter designated seventeen new national monuments and enlarged several others in Alaska on December 1, 1978. Aggregating some fifty-six million acres, the new national monuments doubled the size of the National Park System. Because huge tracts of wilderness were removed from the possibility of private development, many Alaskan citizens became outraged, directing their hatred and condemnation at the agency responsible for managing the newly protected areas—the National Park Service.

For the 1979 late-summer hunting season officials of the service hoped to establish a more visible presence in Alaska. In early June, Area Director John Cook requested that Ranger Bill Tanner develop an interim staffing plan for the recent land acquisitions. With Rick Smith serving as leader, the Alaska Task Force consisted of twenty-two men and women from the "lower forty-eight." Each park ranger had 2.6 million acres to patrol—rugged, inhospitable real estate greater in size than Yellowstone and Grand Teton National Parks combined.

The team members brought considerable experience from their senior-level ranger positions. They had been chosen for their talent with people, proven skill in the field, ability to operate independently, and ability to "think on their feet." All were commissioned law enforcement officers and able to handle themselves in intense, hostile conditions. They would be called on to use every bit of their skills.

As the rangers began to arrive in mid-July to oversee the new monuments, they were greeted with overt hostility by the locals. While not every Alaskan was bitter and some even welcomed the rangers, the prevailing political and social climate was uncomfort-

Ironically, eighteen months after this photo was taken, ranger Dave Mihalic was to return to this spot (Yukon-Charley Rivers National Preserve) and serve for the next four years as the area's first superintendent. DAVE MIHALIC COLLECTION

able at best. State newspapers demanded that the National Park Service leave, and negative editorials and lopsided articles flourished. Redneck and barroom boasting persisted, and statements such as "there are people out there who'd as soon shoot you as look at you" were common. Not easily intimidated, the ranger team demonstrated its law enforcement skill by winning five of six marksmanship medals at the Alaska Police Olympics.

During air patrol flights, the team was always alert to "pot shots" from the ground, sitting on their bulletproof vests and insisting that their pilot sit on two! Some businesses refused to provide services to the team (a ranger with an impacted tooth was denied dental treatment in Anchorage), a friend of one of the group was assaulted, and several task force members were forced to leave rented quarters when the landlady received a bomb threat. As the tension increased, things turned uglier. Five bullets pierced the window of the NPS area director's office during the night. Animosity peaked on September 11, when an arsonist destroyed a charter plane being used by a team for patrol.

Despite this considerable opposition, however, the rangers of the Alaska Task Force were able to successfully accomplish the job they were sent to do—patrolling huge areas, establishing an authority and presence where none had previously existed, enforcing the law, attending public meetings, and answering many questions about the new parklands.

One of the most rewarding jobs a ranger does is search and rescue (SAR). The Grand Canyon averages hundreds of SARs every year, including saving victims of river rafting, hiking, climbing, flying, and driving as well as suicides, heart attacks, and snake bites.
AUTHOR'S COLLECTION

UNITED STATES PARK POLICE

The United States Park Police is an important and separate section of the National Park Service, with law enforcement responsibility primarily in and around the metropolitan region of the District of Columbia.

As employees of the second oldest uniformed federal law enforcement agency in the nation (the United States Customs Service, founded in 1789, is older), the Park Police trace their history to 1791, when President George Washington created the Park Watchmen. Washington called upon these special officers to serve in and around the many public reservations in the District of Columbia. Park Watchmen patrolled the grounds of the Capitol, the White House, and other significant buildings and areas within the capital of the new nation.

With U.S. Park Police pilot Don Usher at the controls, officer Mel Windsor pulls in one of the five survivors of Air Florida Flight 90 after it crashed into the frozen Potomac River on January 13, 1982. U.S. PARK POLICE/CHARLES PEREIRA PHOTO

In 1849, management of the Park Watchmen was moved to the Department of the Interior, and then to the United States Army Corps of Engineers in 1867. Fifteen years later, Congress gave the Park Watchmen "the same powers and duties as the Metropolitan Police of the District," and in 1919 renamed the force the United States Park Police. In 1933, President Franklin D. Roosevelt placed them "under the exclusive charge and control of the director of the National Park Service."

Officers of the United States Park Police (and park rangers) are among the few federal law enforcement officials trained to perform "street" duties similar to metropolitan police departments. Their functions and powers are the same as those of the local police and they also have environmentally oriented responsibilities for parklands. The park police jurisdiction includes areas in the District of Columbia, Maryland, and Virginia. The approximately

625 park police officers wear distinctive blue uniforms, very similar to those of traditional city police departments, and are supported by civilian personnel. Officers not only routinely assist tourists and help lost children, they respond to a wide range of law enforcement situations including traffic violations, accidents, homicides, shootings, rapes, drug abuse, assaults, and acts of domestic violence, among others.

Employing several helicopters, Park Police provide search, rescue, and advanced emergency medical assistance to the region, both inside and outside their jurisdiction. With their broad authority and quick mobility, they have been detailed to many national situations, including the September 11 terrorist attack in 2001, the 1996 Olympics in Atlanta and subsequent bombing investigation, the 1993 Los Angeles riot after the Rodney King trial, and the 1980 Cuban Refugee Crisis in Florida. They routinely assist in providing both air and ground escort to the President of the United States as he moves about the Washington, D.C. area.

When Reverend Martin Luther King Jr. gave his "I Have a Dream" speech on the steps of the Lincoln Memorial on August 28, 1963, Gordon Gundrum, a uniformed National Park Ranger stood just behind him, providing security and assistance.

In 1973, the United States Park Police began serving New York City's Gateway National Recreation Area and the Golden Gate National Recreation Area in San Francisco, primarily due to the largely urban nature of the two areas. There are now Park Police contingents at the Presidio in San Francisco and at Fort Wadsworth and the Statue of Liberty in New York City. Officers provide technical assistance to field rangers by staffing most of the National Park Service's seven regional offices with law enforcement specialists.

CAPTURING
CHARLES MANSON

Satan incarnate, Charles Manson and The Family may never have been brought to justice but for the tenacity and skill of rangers in Death Valley National Monument.

On August 9, 1969, a pregnant Sharon Tate and four friends were butchered in her exclusive Los Angeles-area home. Late the following night, Leo and Rosemary LaBianca met the same horrible fate. Selected at random, the seven innocent victims were guilty of nothing more than just being home.

An evil Charles Manson, along with his mindless, drug-crazed followers, had committed some of the most gruesome murders in California history. Ultimately, they were convicted in the then-longest trial in the annals of American crime. They were linked to a dozen homicides and unsolved disappearances, and their bizarre web of terror included arson, burglary, armed robbery, vehicle theft, drugs, child abuse, rape, illegal firearms, and attempted murder.

In the remote northwestern corner of Death Valley is the Racetrack. A dry lake bed several miles in diameter, it is one of the most tortured, arid spots of North America reachable by vehicle. A maze of faded side roads, abandoned mines, and rocky canyons, it is perfect for society's dropouts and misfits. Here, dozens of miles from any prying eye, Charles Manson wantonly set fire to the park's new front-end loader, parked on the area's one graded road. That costly act of vandalism on September 19, 1969, marked the beginning of the end for The Manson Family and its psychotic leader.

Within hours of the crime, based on key information from a nearby camper and several other clues doggedly gleaned from the stark area by a team of determined park rangers, an All Points Bulletin was issued for a red pickup seen in the area the night before. One set of vehicle tracks found at the arson scene was distinctive enough to be quickly linked to a standard four-wheel-drive Toyota. But the little truck, along with its ragtag band of hippies, had disappeared in the shadowy heart of the rugged desert.

In this isolated tract of rock and sand people are often remembered, particularly a curious tribe of mostly young girls. Slowly but tenaciously, a small task force of park authorities and local law-enforcement officials followed a convoluted trail of evidence and their own intuitive guesses. Ranger Dick Powell and California Highway Patrolman Jim Pursell, the two key officers, were joined by others from their own agencies as well as the offices of the Inyo County Attorney and Sheriff, as well as California Fish and Game.

For the next three weeks, the team pursued an incredibly involved investigation; each day revealed more pieces to their odd puzzle. The list of crimes soon grew far broader than just the destruction of government property; it now included numerous stolen cars, major theft, firearms, drugs, and a sizable count of underage children. Finally, on October 10 and 12, 1969, twenty-six people were taken into custody at the Barker Ranch, an abandoned homestead just yards outside the park at the inhospitable southern end of Death Valley. Manson, Leslie Van Houten, "Squeaky" Fromme, Susan Atkins, and Linda

Kasabian, among others, were jailed. Over the next few weeks, the shocking connection between the Manson Family and the horrific Tate-LaBianca murders would slowly surface.

THE *1970* "YOSEMITE RIOT": A MILESTONE CRISIS FOR RANGERS

"Rangers are being attacked and surrounded and they need all the help they can get." This 7:35 P.M. message to a local sheriff from a Yosemite radio dispatcher defines the exact moment the National Park Service law enforcement program "came of age."

Park rangers come largely from non-police backgrounds, attracted by the agency mission and the fragile resources they swear to protect. Before 1970 most received a modicum of one- and two-day law enforcement courses, generally sprinkled over a long career. Practical police skills required for the "street" were gained on the job. Some citations may have been issued for minor offenses, but few rangers ever needed to execute a physical arrest. On their first day, their supervisor probably issued them a beat-up citation book, a stiff pair of steel handcuffs, and with any luck, six rounds of .38 caliber ammunition in a World War II (rather than World War I) revolver, housed in a well-worn holster. Traditional, "old school" park managers—afraid of negative public opinion—strictly dictated this defensive equipment be kept out of view, locked in a glove compartment or stuffed deep into a briefcase. And for most rangers of that era that was sufficient . . . until the urban ills of the late 1960s seeped into the national parks.

Viet Nam, Kent State, Watergate, and Woodstock. Drugs, the draft, radicals, and the sexual revolution. Within the previous five years America had suffered over three hundred racial riots, and Black Panthers became a household name. We were concerned about the environment and twenty million of us showed up at the first Earth Day. On more socially radical college campuses such as Stanford and Berkeley, a counter-culture, anti-establishment era was in full bloom. A "back-to-nature" climate existed that brought young people to rural America in droves, and urban problems painfully exploded. National parks would soon be scarred by disaster, and the System would be sobered. Yosemite was a place of Volkswagen vans, LSD, and hippies: "Turn on, drop out." It was a "lose-lose" situation for those several dozen rangers who had to endure it.

On the Memorial Day before the riot, Yosemite rangers experienced an increased number of younger visitors from the San Francisco area, resulting in a significant skirmish. Officials worked twelve hours a day, seven days a week. Park radio traffic was continuous, and harried patrolmen raced from one crisis to the next. Quasi-legal roadblocks were set up at the entrance stations and mechanical inspections were randomly conducted on every third or fourth vehicle. Tempers flared as vehicles queued. Unescorted adolescents were often refused entry for such things as no taillight; if admitted, they had to prove ample money to take care of themselves.

The week prior to the riot, the park was hectic: seven people drowned or died climbing, and rangers issued 151 citations and arrested fifty-seven people—including twenty-three minors—for disorderly conduct, intoxication, stolen property, and drugs. Local FBI intelligence accurately suggested a serious confrontation was brewing for the upcoming holiday—a peaceful communion with nature would soon become a hellish experience.

The first major hint at trouble that three-day July 4 weekend occurred Friday night when the local sheriff heard that rangers were confronting unruly crowds gathered in the meadows and nearby campgrounds. Mainstream family America—the "straights" who paid the $3 for a campsite—could not sleep, many because they were afraid.

Roving bands of half-naked hippies swaggered from one family tent to the next, panhandling money and food. Rock music blared and despite extreme fire danger, fireworks exploded in the dark. Gatherings of juveniles shouted obscenities to the next tribal enclave, the second group trying to outdo the first in vulgarity and loudness. Vehicles raced throughout the valley; loud mufflers thundered off the granite walls. A routine ranger campground patrol often resulted in rocks being thrown; anyone in uniform was fair game for verbal assaults. To those officials out taking the park's pulse that night, the Valley's almost primitive, jungle-like atmosphere was surrealistic and nerve-wracking. More wine and drugs and the momentum for a nightmare kept building.

At 5:20 P.M. that Saturday, a highly concerned Yosemite ranger staff alerted neighboring counties that it faced major problems, but no help was actually requested for the unrest. Word was out there would be a huge, protest-type gathering in Stoneman Meadow, an open grassy area in the center of the Village. Notice-of-Closure signs were hurriedly posted for 7:00 P.M. and, as dusk approached, four hundred to five hundred people gathered. Psychedelic peace symbols, love beads, and long hair predominated. Despite the agency's "line in the sand," people kept on drinking, smoking "weed," and stockpiling baseball-sized rocks. A ranger with a bullhorn tried to clear the field and used "impact on the meadow" as the pretext for dispersing revelers. Along with numerous officials on foot, sixteen riders on horseback began sweeping the field, some even trying to lasso the hippies. A slow "charge" was underway and at first it was somewhat orderly; a few people even left.

It was soon realized, however, that the "tree fuzz" were largely unarmed and greatly outnumbered. Rocks flew while bottles were broken over the faces of the horses; the rout began, and a mob quickly became vicious. Park employees had to flee for their lives. Hell-raising in Stoneman Meadow continued while the Service frantically called for help.

Before dawn, nearly 150 officers from the FBI, Border Patrol, Marshal's Office, California Highway Patrol, the state's Office of Emergency Services, and sheriffs' deputies and policemen from five nearby counties responded, many from as much as three hours away. All non-federal officers were sworn in as Deputy United States Marshals, including—mistakenly—one locally convicted cattle rustler temporarily released from a jail cell to assist. Handed a gun, he rode to the melee with a sheriff.

Ambushed by rioters, two police cars were destroyed and two deputies needed to fire into the air and brandish their shotguns to escape; both needed medical attention. Staff from the park hospital also treated numerous bloodied hippies; fortunately none were seriously injured. As one veteran ranger stated, "It is a miracle that people weren't killed." At least 149 arrests were made, with the mostly young prisoners bused to Fresno and Madera jails.

The "Yosemite Riot" overwhelmingly validated a need for a professional law enforcement program for National Park Rangers.

RANGERS RESPOND TO TERRORISM

The National Park Service and its employees answered the September 11, 2001 "Attack On America" in an unprecedented fashion. Director Fran Mainella quickly pledged full support of the agency's resources and within hours, both

*The Statue of Liberty, possibly this country's most enduring symbol of freedom, was
immediately secured after the September 11, 2001, attack on America.*
NATIONAL PARK SERVICE, STATUE OF LIBERTY NATIONAL MONUMENT ARCHIVES

the Service's National Type I Incident Management Team and United States
Park Police Chief's Command Post were activated, overseeing an immediate
and unified response: "Operation Secure Parks." Safety of our country's greatest symbols of freedom, such as the Liberty Bell, White House, Statue of Liberty, Mount Rushmore, USS *Arizona*, Lincoln Memorial, the Arch in St. Louis,
and Washington Monument, became paramount.

That first day, national parks in New York City, Boston, Philadelphia, and
Washington, D.C. closed down as soon as the threat was recognized. The Park
Police provided escorts to both the President and the Secretary of State as well
as evacuated the Secretary of the Interior. Park Police helicopter pilots flew critically injured people from the Pentagon while rangers mobilized on the National Mall. Park crews in agency boats aided the Coast Guard in guarding
bridges leading into New York City and they transported firefighters from New
Jersey to aid at the Twin Tower crash site in Manhattan.

All across America, the National Park Service provided critical assistance. Rangers in Florida secured beaches to safeguard the space shuttle and performed perimeter control for a nuclear power plant. In Hawaii, they controlled a road to a vital radar site for the Federal Aviation Administration. Fort Point National Historic Site was temporarily closed down due to its proximity to the Golden Gate Bridge. Around-the-clock, rangers guarded (and still do) eight of this country's largest dams, including Hoover, Glen Canyon, Shasta, and Coulee. They worked with the Federal Emergency Management Agency in New Jersey, New York, and Washington, D.C., and soon were asked to be sky marshals.

During the year following the attack, one-third of the agency's fifteen hundred law enforcement rangers saw duty outside their parks. At any given time, even at the end of 2002, approximately eighty rangers were still away from home, assigned to nearly twenty high-risk sites around the country,

The Service has Special Events Teams (SETs), which respond to situations requiring crowd and/or crisis management. This Western Region SET spent seven weeks at Mt. Rushmore in 1991 in response to threats against the monument during a planned speech by President Bush.
PAUL HENRY COLLECTION

including strategic dams; the President's retreat at Camp David; and Main Interior Building in Washington, D.C. At this writing, the NPS has spent more than fifty thousand man-days in this effort.

A further reflection of this country's concern for preparedness was the Service's role in the XIX Winter Olympics in Salt Lake City in 2002. Approximately 150 employees spent seventeen days providing security and visitor information. At the request of the Secret Service, one hundred law enforcement rangers with winter and snow expertise assisted with perimeter control in the rugged settings of four outdoor athletic venues. They often worked the midnight shift, traveling by ski, snowshoe, and snowmobile.

Rangers were well-recognized for their expertise by both the Secret Service and officials of the Olympics. The national news routinely spotlighted this winter and snow prowess as well as routinely gave credit to those men and women who provided a quality interpretive contact at the Games' visitor centers and information booths.

Ranger Michael Smithson leads an interpretive tour at Rocky Mountain National Park in the summer of 1985. BILL SONTAG PHOTO

Chapter 11
HOW DO YOU BECOME A RANGER?

If nothing else, those hoping to become park rangers must be persistent. Because positions are limited and breaking into the government system can be difficult, patience and perseverance are essential for the national park job seeker.

There are two types of positions—permanent and seasonal—and differing federal rules and regulations govern each. Permanent jobs usually require a higher level of education and training, and more experience. Further, the various ranger job classifications, such as protection, interpretation, and resource management, have different requirements for education and skills.

Special consideration for government positions is given to those who have served in the Armed Forces, and this has been the case since the Civil War. To be entitled to any preference, a veteran must meet well-defined eligibility requirements. Having served honorably in the Armed Forces can be very helpful in gaining employment as either a permanent or seasonal ranger.

PERMANENT

People become park rangers on a regular basis, but there is no "normal" way of doing so. Today's applicant needs at least a college degree to be competitive (though one is not technically required for most positions), and an advanced degree is a real plus. Unless one is applying for a specialty job (in archeology or wildlife management, for example), the subject matter of course work is not particularly important.

The key to landing a permanent ranger position is to attain permanent "status" in the civilian federal government. It is so important that many prospective

Future President Gerald Ford, a seasonal ranger in Yellowstone in 1936.
NATIONAL PARK SERVICE, YELLOWSTONE NATIONAL PARK ARCHIVES

rangers will take their first federal jobs with another agency, such as the Corps of Engineers or the Internal Revenue Service. Other routes for gaining "status" include the Peace Corps, Outstanding Scholar, and Student Career Experience programs. Some aspirants have worked into permanent jobs by becoming "clerks-typists" with the National Park Service. After a year of federal employment, would-be rangers can apply for any position for which they qualify.

SEASONAL

Unlike permanent positions, there actually is a specific procedure to become a seasonal ranger. Most jobs are for less than four months, although there are exceptions. There is a well-defined application system for those desiring to become seasonal rangers. Applicants must submit their forms for processing during the first three months of the calendar year. Prospective rangers may specify up to four park areas where they would like to work, and competition is keen for the more popular parks. For this reason, it is often easier to find employment in lesser-known park units. Initial screening of candidates is done in central offices and at individual parks. Each area will review and ultimately hire as needed; how one person compares to another is determined by ranking criteria formulated in the park.

The National Park Service would be crippled without dedicated seasonal employees.
LARRY FREDERICK COLLECTION

One additional tip for those hoping to find work as seasonal rangers: placing a "face with a name" often makes it easier for supervisors to hire someone. Therefore, working in a national park as a volunteer, as a student assistant, or for a concessioner might make the difference between becoming a ranger and not. And remember that when it comes to working in the national parks, success comes through persistence.

NATIONAL PARK
RANGER ACADEMIES

The Yosemite School of Field Natural History was founded in 1925 by Dr. Harold Bryant and began as a six-week session for field naturalists (interpreters).

Finally discontinued in 1953, this was the Service's first official long-term training course. Park rangers will generally attend one or more of the following extended academies during their careers.

Horace M. Albright
Training Center

The National Park Service Training Center Program was launched in Yosemite National Park; the first class of rangers began on September 23, 1957. Students, under tutelage of Frank Kowski, the Service's "Mr. Training," attended "An Introduction to National Park Service Operations" for three months. At this time, participants were seasoned with at least a few years of field experience. On October 26, 1963, a permanent center was dedicated on the South Rim of Grand Canyon National Park and several generations of rangers began their National Park Service careers there. Named for the Service's second director, the Horace M. Albright Training Center has been at the forefront of federal training ever since. Currently, the agency's newer employees attend an eight-week-long "Rangers Skills" course. Through a broad variety of both short and long courses, more than thirty thousand students have experienced quality learning at the facility.

Stephen T. Mather
Training Center

Named after the first National Park Service director, the Stephen T. Mather Training Center at Harpers Ferry National Historical Park in West Virginia opened its doors in 1964. The small campus is principally housed in Anthony Hall, a Union Army building that President Abraham Lincoln slept in on his way to Antietam in 1862. After the Civil War, the facility became Storer College, and for nearly a century, a home of early African-American higher learning. In 1881, Frederick Douglass delivered his famous speech on John Brown from the Hall's front porch, and in 1906 the groundwork for the National Association for Advancement of Colored People was laid there. It is fitting that interpreters, those National Park Service employees most intimately involved with history and this country's heritage, train there. In addition to sharpening the skills of interpreters, training at Mather now includes other disciplines such as administration and cultural resources management. Approximately

Yosemite rangers are training in this 1923 mock cliff rescue. Left to right: Forest Townsley, Henry Skeleton, Charlie Adair, John Wagner, and John Bingaman. The "victim" is unknown. Note the size of the rope. MRS. JOHN BINGAMAN COLLECTION

100,000 students have utilized a wide range of Mather Training Center courses down through the years.

Federal Law Enforcement Training Center

The Treasury Law Enforcement Officers Training School (TLEOTS) opened in Washington, D.C. in 1951. By 1967 it "was the best there was in the federal government." After recognizing the need for coordinated, standardized training for all federal police officers, the Consolidated Federal Law Enforcement Training Center (CFLETC) was finally authorized on June 30, 1970. TLEOTS became CFLETC. Five rangers first attended a basic United States Park Police School in the summer of 1970, as did others intermittently after this time, but within a few short years, all park rangers having law enforcement duties were attending the more elaborate Treasury school.

Park rangers with police functions as part of their responsibility must graduate from the eighteen-week standardized training of the Federal Law Enforcement Training Center ("Consolidated" was eventually dropped from the title and the school is now known as the FLETC). Consisting of two thousand acres, it is located at Glynco, an abandoned Naval air field in Southern Georgia. Except for the Federal Bureau of Investigation (FBI) and the Drug Enforcement Agency (DEA), all seventy-four other federal agencies with law enforcement responsibilities utilize this FLETC facility. Since the National Park Service began participating at the Center, some twenty-five hundred rangers have graduated, many achieving the very highest honors of their class.

Seasonal Law Enforcement Training Programs

Since at least 1923, when seasonal rangers in Yellowstone first began receiving training, "temporaries" may have obtained a few days' worth of instruction in their park at the beginning of each visitor season. If they were lucky, this preparation might have been a whole week in length. For those in protection this included not only law enforcement, but likely other skills, such as basic fire fighting, search and rescue, first aid, and general park information. For

Yosemite rangers receive instruction in 1940 on using a recently designed stretcher for evacuating the injured from the ski slopes of Badger Pass.
NATIONAL PARK SERVICE, YOSEMITE NATIONAL PARK RESEARCH LIBRARY

naturalists, the training would be equally as brief and broad. By necessity, all seasonal rangers had to be masters of on-the-job-training.

The first servicewide Seasonal Law Enforcement School was in June 1971, at Harpers Ferry, West Virginia, and consisted of one hundred hours of police training. It was sporadic after this. In March 1978, the country's first land management seasonal law enforcement academy opened in Santa Rosa, California. By January 2003, its 104th class had graduated, with nearly twenty-six hundred students successfully completing since it started. In the early 1990s, there were twenty-one of these academies, and over time there have been at least thirty-seven; at the end of 2002, however, eleven remained nationwide. All are affiliated with colleges and universities. Each school session is a minimum of 285 hours of police training and, although autonomous of the National Park Service, the agency does provide curriculum oversite, review, and coordination.

How Much Does a Ranger Earn?

Galen Clark, who became Yosemite's first "Guardian" in 1866, received a salary "not to exceed five hundred dollars per annum." Yellowstone National Park Gamekeeper Harry Yount, often recognized as the federal government's first ranger, earned $1000 for his year's work in 1880. To systematize the salary scale, the Secretary of the Interior approved three categories of rangers in 1902. A Class 1 ranger was paid $90 per month, and Class 2 and 3 rangers earned $75 and $50 respectively (but all rangers had to provide their own riding stock, weapons, and supplies).

For the next two decades, basic ranger salaries varied from park to park. In 1910 for example, pay ranged from $900 in Mount Rainier to $1,500 in Sequoia, though ranger duties in both areas were essentially the same. Annual salaries were standardized at $1,500 for chief rangers and $1,350 for Class 1 rangers (permanents) in 1915 with the issuance of "Regulations Governing Rangers In The National Parks" by the Secretary of Interior. Park rangers (like other federal civilian employees) were made subject to the Classification Act of 1949 and their jobs were graded using criteria from the new General Schedule (GS) system. From 1949 until the late 1970s, a full-time park ranger normally began at the GS-5 level.

Today, permanent rangers start their employment with a GS-7 grade and an annual pay rate of about $30,000, and over $34,000 if law enforcement is a central duty. After one year of satisfactory performance, rangers usually are promoted to the GS-9 level, and their salary is boosted by approximately $5,000. Subsequent career promotions and pay are based upon performance. There are ten incremental steps for every GS grade (7, 9, 11, etc.), and salary usually depends on the number of years served at previous levels.

For an idea of what a ranger earned in 2002, here are examples of pay rates for several different National Park Service positions. A GS-5 seasonal interpreter in Olympic National Park makes $24,701 per annum; $45,285 for a GS-11 district ranger in a medium-sized area such as Southern Arizona's Saguaro National Park; and the GS-14 chief ranger in a more complex park such as the Everglades may begin at $76,271. Park administrators (superintendents of the largest parks, for example) in key "Senior Executive Service" positions can earn well over $100,000 per year.

The salary may also be affected by the geographical location in which the employee works; several areas, such as Philadelphia, New York City, San Francisco, and Seattle will have "locality pay" to partially offset higher costs of living.

RANGER ASSOCIATIONS

Association of National Park Rangers

The Association of National Park Rangers is the largest organization in the country working specifically for the concerns and goals of the whole of the National Park Service and all of its many types of employees, despite its singular-sounding name. On September 30, 1977, thirty-three rangers from fourteen different national park areas (and one from the Bureau of Land Management) gathered in Jackson Hole, Wyoming, for a three-day reunion of old friends. They found, however, they shared more than just common interests and decided to form the Association, which is rooted in passion for the ranger and love for the agency. The author was the group's first president.

For nearly three decades, the Association of National Park Rangers has been a strong advocate for both the profession and the agency. Anyone may belong, not just rangers.
AUTHOR'S COLLECTION

With fifteen hundred members from all areas of the country representing most job specialties of the Service, the Association has become a strong, welcome voice for the ranger and a powerful champion of the national park idea. The Association—respected for both its idealism and tempered common sense—has testified before Congress numerous times on major issues such as employee housing, benefits, pay, restructuring, and bureau reform. Its counsel and informed input is continually sought by Congress, the Department of the Interior, and the National Park Service. As the highlight of each year, several hundred of the group gather—in the finest tradition of the legendary nineteenth century mountain men—for a Ranger Rendezvous of camaraderie, business, and exchange, all at their own expense. For more information, contact the ANPR, P.O. Box 108, Larned, KS 67550-0108.

National Association for Interpretation

The National Association for Interpretation (education) was formed in this country in 1988, emerging from two existing organizations created in the 1950s: the Association of Interpretive Naturalists and the Western Interpreters Association. Both of these groups were created to provide training and networking opportunities for professionals in natural and cultural resources and history, in settings such as parks, zoos, nature centers, and museums. With forty-two hundred members in fifty states and twenty-nine nations, the Association provides a focus for those interested in both the art and science of education about resources. About 30 percent of its members are federal employees, 25 percent work for state government, 25 percent for local government, and the rest hold positions with private organizations.

The Association's stated goals are to become the international voice for interpretation, to encourage and promote professional development for students, and to develop and broaden leadership among its members. The highlight of each year is when members gather to exchange information and learn from each other. More than fourteen hundred interested people met at the last conference. In addition to the National Park Service, the group is supported by a diverse range of employers, from Sea World to the California State Park System to the Environmental Protection Agency. For more information, contact the NAI, P.O. Box 2246, Fort Collins, CO 80522.

The George Wright Society

The George Wright Society is "dedicated to the protection, preservation and management of cultural and natural parks and preserves through research and education."

Founded in 1980, it is a nonprofit association of researchers, managers, educators, and other professionals who work on behalf of the scientific and heritage values of the world's parks and protected places. Natural areas are sites of important environmental research and related natural resource management activities and projects. Cultural and historic spots often embody irreplaceable history, archaeology, and other forms of the world's heritage. The challenges facing protected areas today are so complex they can overwhelm any single discipline. The society fosters communication and bolsters a shared purpose for all of those concerned with saving these treasures.

Born in 1904, when conservation was in its infancy, George Melendez Wright roamed the San Francisco Bay area as a child, coming to know and love its plants and animals. In college he studied with famous scientists, including zoologist Joseph Grinnell, and in 1927 became an assistant park naturalist in Yosemite Valley. Blessed with foresight, he argued for our priceless areas to be viewed in a scientific, holistic manner. Using his own money, he soon began

Because of the demands of both the economy and the armed forces during World War II, 1941 was the last year that parks (such as Crater Lake, shown here) operated with full staffs until the end of the decade. NATIONAL PARK SERVICE, CRATER LAKE NATIONAL PARK ARCHIVES

funding a wildlife survey for the then existing national parks. While working on a commission studying potential new parks along the Mexican border in 1936, he died in an automobile accident. Had he lived, he likely would have become one of America's foremost conservationists. A highlight every other year is the conference; more than six hundred people attended the most recent one, with approximately 40 percent of the Society coming from outside the United States. For more information, contact the GWS, P.O. Box 65, Hancock, MI 49930-0065.

How Do You
Become a Ranger?

Shown here in 1917, this soldier and ranger patrol station at Norris in Yellowstone was dedicated as the Museum of the National Park Ranger on the service's seventy-fifth anniversary in 1991. NATIONAL PARK SERVICE, YELLOWSTONE NATIONAL PARK ARCHIVES

Museum of the National Park Ranger

Located in Yellowstone National Park, the museum traces the history of the ranger profession from its early roots in the military to the present day and "honors the tradition and contribution of all employees of the National Park Service."

The museum consists of several rooms of displays, photographs, and original memorabilia. It also houses replicated interiors of both an early-day soldier and ranger station. Constructed in 1908, the present building is the third on the site, all of which were used by the Army until it left in 1918. The facility then served as a ranger station until 1959, when the Hebegen Lake Earthquake rendered it unsafe to live in.

The building was renovated and fitted with displays with money from several different sources, including a gift of $250,000 from the Continental Oil Company (CONOCO), $300,000 provided by the National Park Service, and donations from the Association of National Park Rangers, as well as others. It was dedicated on August 25, 1991, the NPS's seventy-fifth anniversary. Each year twenty-two thousand people visit the museum, and admission is free. Open only during the summer and staffed mostly by retired Service employees volunteering their time, the Museum of the National Park Ranger is at Norris Junction, twenty-one miles south of the Yellowstone Park Headquarters at Mammoth.

International Ranger Federation

Park rangers, wardens, and managers on six continents are dedicated and compassionate about the special treasures in their care. The challenges facing these men and women at the national, state, and local levels of the approximately thirty thousand protected areas around the world grow exceedingly more complex: from game poachers killing wardens in Kenya to drug lords taking over national parks in Columbia, to just putting "Guardaparques" in Bolivia into uniforms. Often these people compete with desperate, poverty-stricken villagers living on the fringe of their area. Many custodians of our global wealth, particularly those in Third World Countries, have few resources available.

Created on August 1, 1992, the Federation is the only international organization representing the field ranger profession. At the Third Congress of the Federation held in Kruger National Park in South Africa in September, 2000, more than 350 rangers and park representatives from at least fifty different countries, including the author, met to share ideas and mutual concerns. For further information, contact the International Ranger Federation c/o ANPR, P.O. Box 108, Larned, KS 67550-0108.

"NINETY-DAY WONDERS": SEASONAL RANGERS

At the height of the summer—peak season for most, but not all, park areas—there are approximately twenty-six thousand employees working for the National Park Service. Almost eight thousand of these people are temporary and include laborers, clerks, truck drivers, aids, trail crew, maintenance, dispatchers, firefighters, and rangers. These seasonal employees are truly the "backbone" of the Service, and the agency would be crippled without them.

In the "off season" this number of temporary workers drops to about four thousand. In a seasonal park such as Glacier, there may be three hundred seasonals in the summer, but possibly only thirty during the winter. These figures swell or shrink depending on the agency's overall budget and how money is allocated and used by individual parks and programs. The seasonals are students, teachers on vacation, people choosing temporary employment as a lifestyle, those who would like to work longer but can't, and younger men and women struggling to launch a federal career by getting "a foot in the door."

This Yosemite ranger was free to use any one of five different uniform suppliers from around the country in 1920. Prices ranged from $37.50 to $62.75.

When Yellowstone's first gamekeeper Harry Yount resigned in 1881, he wrote that the park needed *"a small and reliable police force of men, employed when needed."* That same year C. H. Wyman was appointed an "agent of the government" in Yellowstone for a two-week patrol to prevent vandalism and enforce the rules and regulations. Down through the years there was a smattering of men working in the few park areas. Just like today, their employment was dependent on funding, so these rangers may have worked for just a few months each year. For one month in 1914, Ester Cleveland Brazell was a seasonal guide at Wind Cave National Park, the first woman to hold a ranger-like title.

When automobiles were finally officially permitted in national parks (1908 in Mount Rainier and 1913 in Sequoia and Yosemite), travel patterns and related impacts to resources changed drastically. It was not long before ordinary families could take extended vacations in the parks of the West, mostly when school was out. Visitors increasingly now came during the summer and had to be accommodated. Prior to this time, park managers did not have to be so focused on when work was done; employment and accomplishing the job was limited by budgets. In response to these changing touring habits, as an example, seven of the ten seasonal rangers hired in Yosemite in the summer of 1914 for entrance station duty were from the University of California. Teachers and college students were largely available these three months, and any ranger working just during the park's short primary travel season was often labeled a "ninety-day wonder."

NOTE

There are several generations of men and women who worked seasonally for the National Park Service as fee collectors, fire lookouts, interpreters, backcountry patrolmen, and in other positions, who fondly reflect on their very rewarding days as "ninety-day wonders."

Glacier's rustic and remote Indian Ridge Lookout served as a late summer and early fall home to rangers in the early history of the park. NATIONAL PARK SERVICE, GLACIER NATIONAL PARK ARCHIVES

Chapter 12
THE RANGER LIFE

PLACES RANGERS LIVE

Among the benefits of being a ranger are the wonderful places you get to call home. A good example is a quaint old lighthouse at road's end, with the Golden Gate Bridge and skyline of San Francisco poking above the fog as backdrop. Another is a gatekeeper's stone carriage house, rustically nestled in a maple-fir forest near Maine's rocky coast. A ranger may have two-thousand-foot-high red sandstone cliffs, sparkling white sand dunes, a hardwood forest, or the highest peak in North America in his or her backyard, and spot a grizzly, alligator, flamingo, elk, or eagle on the walk to work.

While the settings may be beautiful, the reality of the living situations are often less than ideal. There are a number of rangers (and families) who can reach their homes only by airplane, boat, snowmobile, or four-wheel-drive vehicle. And when they arrive home, they may be in tents, fire towers, houseboats, Army Quonset huts, metal shipping crates, or wooden shacks condemned decades before. Housing locations also may be without roads, indoor plumbing, neighbors, and electricity. The nearest store or doctor may be days and many airline-miles away (weather permitting!).

The remoteness and lack of amenities can take its toll. As one veteran wife of a chief ranger recently said, "The National Park ideal is not just a job, it is a way of life, a passion. But the price is sometimes very high. It is hard on families and the divorce rate is high. Being paid in 'beautiful sunsets' is wonderful, but the difficulties of the lifestyle sometimes cloud those sunsets."

Duty stations can be in unlikely and extraordinary places. The ranger outpost at Anaktuvuk Pass is 160 miles above the Arctic Circle, the farthest north and one of the most remote in the National Park System. Rangers also live

This and several similar tents, located at the 14,000-foot level, serve as a short-lived "ranger station." This one is also used by a rotating team of physicians who aid mountaineers seeking the summit of Alaska's 20,320-foot-high Mt. McKinley.
NATIONAL PARK SERVICE, DENALI NATIONAL PARK ARCHIVES

Anacapa Island, home for park rangers of Channel Islands National Park. For most of the 1980s, park rangers actually lived in large metal shipping crates ("containers") on the park's San Miguel Island, sixty-five miles off the coast of California.
NATIONAL PARK SERVICE, CHANNEL ISLANDS NATIONAL PARK ARCHIVES

inside the Arctic Circle at places like Bettles, Kotzebue, and Cold-foot. Below the equator, rangers live on 212-mile-square Guam and work at the seven units of the War in the Pacific National Historical Park, as well as on Saipan, a speck just east of the International Date Line. There are seven separate park service sites in Hawaii, and four parks in the Virgin Islands.

At Lake Powell, young rangers use to live on tiny houseboats deep in secluded side canyons of Southern Utah, at least three hours by fast patrol boat from the nearest paved road. The floating homes were anchored in deep water and heated by a generator. These are some of the most isolated year-round ranger duty stations in the continental United States. A computer-mapping company recently determined that Yellowstone's Thorofare Ranger Station is the "most remote spot in the Lower 48." It takes two days by horse to reach the ranger's summer home there. When the wooden front door of the log outpost is bolted shut at the end of the season, hundreds of large, potentially-painful nails point outward to keep ravenous grizzly bears from breaking it down.

One superintendent recently lived through a winter in Alaska's Wrangell-St. Elias National Park when the wind chill often reached minus 80 degrees. Several years later, he moved to Death Valley where he watched the thermometer hit 122 in the shade—remarkably, the temperature spread between the two locations was over 200 degrees.

ISOLATION AND A RANGER'S SPOUSE

Wives—and an increasing number of husbands—of rangers serving remote duty in our parks and monuments commonly demonstrate real toughness in surviving the unique rigors of isolation. Rangers and their spouses in these select places need to be flexible and self-sufficient. Says one, "We never know when that midnight knock on the door will bring a victim of a car wreck or report of a child lost from the campground. Our best laid plans may have to change at a moment's notice, and often we can't take our days off—for weeks on end." Not all park service couples can handle this demanding lifestyle. Divorces are, unfortunately, relatively common, and suicides have occurred on occasion.

Julie Mossman and her ranger-husband Rick are posted in an isolated section of Yellowstone National Park. Recently Julie's standard "just another day in paradise" experience took an unexpected turn. As six fire trucks stood in her yard, falling ash from a major fire roaring toward them settled on her sons' swing set. Sprinklers, hurriedly placed on top of her sixty-year-old house, sprayed water

Believing in the power of advertising in 1901, these men were in an isolated part of Montana that would soon become Glacier National Park.
NATIONAL PARK SERVICE, GLACIER NATIONAL PARK ARCHIVES

from the nearby Snake River onto the tinder-dry building. Yellow-shirted firefighters, weary from a month's worth of twelve-hour days, were preparing a last-ditch fight to save the dozen historic structures and the ranger station.

With her two young children already safely gone from the area, Julie readied to evacuate her home at South Entrance.

The Mossmans' existence is characterized by isolation. Julie must use a snowmobile to get her small kids to school and together with children their own age. "In the winter, I snowmobile the kids almost three unplowed miles to a car we leave at the end of the maintained road," she says. Often this highway is not yet scraped, and eight inches of overnight snow in Yellowstone is common. "I then drive another fifteen icy miles to their bus stop, which is still another ten miles from school. Twice a day. This speaks nothing to all of the precautionary trips we make to the doctor each winter because I was afraid an ear infection or strep throat might crop up in the middle of the night or over a weekend."

In between chauffeuring children, Julie will transport her trash and garbage out to the same plowed road by the same snow machine, as well as drive thirty miles to pick up mail. The nearest gas station for three months is forty miles away, and, needing to drive more than three hundred miles a week just for school, "keeping the tank full is tricky."

Julie and Rick rarely complain, however, since they know that others in the park have it harder. Some must leave home and move up to headquarters for weeks at a time, which means finding places to stay and awkward alterations to household routines. "One family snowmobiled twenty-five miles from Canyon to Mammoth and then drove ninety more miles to Bozeman for Montessori School. Others routinely drive the same ninety miles for everything from ballet to piano lessons to after school sports for their kids."

Before there was home schooling and satellite learning, rangers serving in such isolated places as Yellowstone, Big Bend, or even Yosemite routinely boarded their older children out during the school year. This came at great family expense, both financially and personally.

In some ways, their life in Yellowstone is much easier than what the Mossmans were used to. Before being transferred here, they lived in Yakutat, a windy, wet, and remote fishing village of five hundred people on the shores of the Gulf of Alaska while Rick served as a ranger for both Glacier Bay and Wrangell-St. Elias National Parks. It is a spectacular setting often shrouded in ocean fog, but everything that people need for their day-to-day lives has to come by water or air, since there is no road in from the outside. The area's single street leads nowhere.

"A gallon of milk there cost $7, bread was $4 a loaf, and a head of lettuce was upwards of $5. So when we were in Anchorage, we would stock up for very long

Rangers on TV

For eleven weeks in 1974, national park rangers figured as central characters in a weekly television series on NBC. In a primetime viewing slot, the world of the National Park Service as it unfolded in the imaginary Sierra National Park was broadcast into millions of American homes. Filmed mostly in Yosemite Valley, *Sierra* was modeled after the real-life adventures of Yosemite park rangers.

The Rangers, a made-for-television movie pilot promoting the series, premiered on Christmas Eve of 1973. The next year, from 8:00 to 9:00 each Thursday evening, Chief Ranger Jack Moore and his fun-loving but hardworking staff wrestled with "the conflict between trying to preserve the natural beauty of the wilderness and accommodating the flood of tourists wanting to utilize the resources of the park. The campers, skiers, hikers, and climbers came in all shapes and sizes. Some were friendly, some stubborn, and some nasty and cruel." The show's biggest star was a troublesome but clever bear named Cruncher who consistently outwitted the rangers.

The series was both approved and assisted by the National Park Service, and Park Ranger Jack Morehead was detailed to the production as a full-time consultant. Despite this endorsement and professional guidance, however, *Sierra* suffered from questionable plots, laughable acting, and needy story lines. Executive Producer Robert Cinnader was never able to match the success of his previous two hits, *Adam 12* and *Emergency*. Even John Denver's melodious title song couldn't rescue the series; it was canceled after just one season.

For decades, Hollywood has used national parks (and, occasionally, a ranger) for both movies and television shows. A few of the more remembered feature films involving parks are *Star Wars, The Greatest Story Ever Told, Dangerous Mission, Indiana Jones and the Temple of Doom, Cliffhanger, Butch Cassidy and the Sundance Kid,* and *National Lampoon's Vacation,* as well as television series such as *Death Valley Days, Sea Hunt,* and *Baa Baa Black Sheep,* filmed in the skies above Channel Islands.

Several television series have also highlighted rangers, including *Flipper,* set in the Florida Keys, and *High Mountain Rangers,* starring Robert Conrad. There have been only two series, however, which have focused specifically on *national* park rangers.

Everglades was the first program, it aired for thirty-nine episodes in 1961–1962. Actor Ron Hayes played Lincoln Vale for thirty minutes each week on NBC. Ranger Vale worked out of the Lost River Patrol Station and traveled the 'glades in his airboat, fighting crime and "saving lost children from alligators." Burt Reynolds was one of the "bad guys" that Vale had to deal with in the Florida swamps. Ron Hayes, in television for another thirty years, was featured in several other series including *Lassie* and *The Rounders.* Hayes recently said that filming *Everglades* was a "defining period in my life, prompting a lifelong love of national parks, conservation, and adventure."

periods. I still get nervous if I don't have at least four bottles of syrup and sixty pounds of dog food ferreted away somewhere. We never knew when we would be back, and if you ran out of something, you were pretty much out of luck." A trip to Anchorage, 350 miles away by jet, was a major excursion for the Mossmans.

"A typical Anchorage buying trip first involved reservations for the flights, no later than three weeks in advance to get the cheapest fares. Obviously we

Dr. Harold and Mrs. Amy Bryant in summer quarters in Yosemite in the mid-1920s. Dr. Bryant was largely responsible for the Service's first educational interpretive programs.
NATIONAL PARK SERVICE, YOSEMITE NATIONAL PARK RESEARCH LIBRARY AND ARCHIVES

would try to combine this with some other need, such as seeing a dentist or doctor, like when I was pregnant with our two sons. We would do dry goods first. We'd go armed with strapping tape, black felt-tip markers, pocket knives, and an estimate of how many shipping boxes we needed to buy for mailing home. If it wasn't raining or snowing we would stake out a corner of the store's parking lot and set up a mini-assembly line packing our purchases.

"If the vehicle we had to rent wasn't big enough, one of us would start shuttling finished boxes to the airport's post office to start the shipping process. If the weather was bad—and it often was—we would usually go to a covered parking garage to pack. It was cold but dry. Once we even returned the car for a large van since we had so much stuff. I think our personal record was twenty-seven boxes. Then we had to allow enough time before our flight home to return to the store and get fresh food, which we would take back as luggage in big duffel bags. Instead of being on a monetary budget, we were on a weight budget since we could only have three bags each at seventy pounds apiece. So everything we took off the shelf went onto a running weight tally before it went into the shopping cart. It was always a race to get the frozen items home and put away in time.

"With no doctor or medical facility in Yakutat, all my prenatal visits involved flying out to Anchorage. The last month of pregnancy I had to move there and stay with friends. The week before Thomas was born, we moved to an Air Force base closer to the hospital because the weather was so treacherous and unpredictable. After he was born, we had to stay for two more weeks before we could go back home. For Jackson, I moved to Minneapolis to have him, this time with a two-year-old in tow. From Yakutat, there was no such thing as a quick and easy trip anywhere. Just like here in Yellowstone, you had to be prepared for absolutely anything: hunger, thirst, accidents, boredom, illness, weather, the unexpected, the works. Traveling light is no longer part of your world."

Julie smiled at the recollections. At the very last possible moment, the raging forest fire on the ridge above her Yellowstone home turned and burned the other way.

A ranger patrol along Denali National Park's remote Riley Creek in 1924.
NATIONAL PARK SERVICE, DENALI NATIONAL PARK ARCHIVES

Glacier Bay National Park's largest vessel, the Nunatak, *is a sixty-five-foot surplus Korean War vessel. A critical tool for the staff, it is used to supply headquarters, assist in scientific research, and support rangers on patrol on the outer coast of Alaska.*
NATIONAL PARK SERVICE, GLACIER BAY NATIONAL PARK ARCHIVES

Despite a record snow, the flag is up and it is "business as usual" as rangers try to prevent the collapse of the roof to the West Entrance of Glacier in the winter of 1997. GARY MOSES COLLECTION

WHAT PARK RANGERS DO

There are several hundred different job titles within the National Park Service, all supporting the agency's mission of "protecting the resource and serving the public." They range from gardener to truck driver, clerk to manager. A number of these positions, however, fall into the broad, collective category of National Park Ranger. The title "ranger" encompasses perhaps more diverse functions and responsibilities than does any other within the federal government. Below are some routine ranger duties:

- Perform search and rescue
- Consult on environmental policies
- Enforce federal, state, and local laws
- Provide emergency medical services
- Fly planes, pilot boats, and SCUBA dive
- Fight structural fires and manage wildland fires

- Give interpretive talks and lead overnight walks
- Manage threatened and endangered plants and animals
- Act as coroners and Immigration and Naturalization officers
- Staff information booths and communication centers
- Perform criminal and internal investigations
- Record history and take oral interviews
- Do light maintenance and construction
- Raise the flag and operate elevators
- Research and collect scientific data
- Train people and write manuals
- Pick up litter and clean latrines
- Monitor air and water quality
- Shoe horses and pack mules
- Investigate accidents
- Operate jails
- Supervise
- Design websites
- Serve as "dog catchers"
- Oversee concession operations
- Intercept drugs and illegal aliens
- Serve as public information specialists
- Take snow surveys and control avalanches
- Do archeology, geology, and paleontology
- Map caves and seal abandoned mine shafts
- Document historical buildings and cultural landscapes
- Administer cemeteries, memorials, and shrines
- Issue filming permits and utility right-of-ways
- Monitor marine debris and survey for fish

Parks are increasingly attracting those adventurers wishing to "push the envelope" by challenging themselves. More people means more emergencies.
MIKE GAUTHIER PHOTO

Grand Canyon's helicopter "210" performing a short-haul evacuation of passengers from a commercial raft stranded on a rock in the Colorado River in June 1991.
KEN PHILLIPS PHOTO

- Collect fees and operate entrance stations
- Manage campgrounds and visitor centers
- Oversee oil, gas, and mineral operations
- Provide living history demonstrations
- Curate museums and maintain archives
- Perform health and safety inspections
- Combat night sky and noise pollution
- Manage wilderness and scenic rivers

Ranger Mark Buktenica at the controls of a one-person sub in Crater Lake in 1988. For three summers, park researchers collected information on the warm hydrothermal vents at the bottom of the deepest lake (1,950 feet) in the United States.
JIM MILESTONE PHOTO

UNDERWATER RANGERS

Some of the best preserved historic shipwrecks in the United States are found in national park areas. Not counting parks in Alaska, the National Park System encompasses over two million acres of submerged lands, an area as large as Yellowstone. At least sixty-one Service sites have significant underwater natural and cultural resources. Over the years, the National Park Service has developed an expertise in studying and recovering artifacts from its underwater resources. In the fall of 1934, for example, the first underwater archeological work in North America (perhaps the world) to use artificial air was undertaken at Virginia's Colonial National Historical Park. Artifacts were recovered from British warships of Cornwallis' fleet, sunk in the York River in 1781.

The National Park Service developed the first non-military diving team in the federal government shortly after Ranger Jack Morehead was certified in SCUBA in 1959. Today, there are about 150 Park Service employees who engage in diving for search and rescue, maintenance, law enforcement, resources management, or some other program.

Along with these talented and dedicated divers, the NPS also employs the nation's only federal team of underwater archeologists at the Submerged Resources Center. Begun in 1976, the center was developed to help with the government's National Reservoir Inundation Study, which required land-management agencies to assess the impact of archeological sites threatened by dams.

Stan Jones wrote many other songs, including the soundtrack for the 1950s TV series Cheyenne, *and "Wringle Wrangle" for the movie* Westward Ho, the Wagons *with actor Fess Parker. He also played the deputy in another 1950s TV series,* Sheriff of Cochise.

The Singing Ranger

Stanley Davis Jones was a national park ranger for just a few years, but he certainly left his mark—in the music business, that is. He was responsible for writing one of the most familiar and best loved country-western songs of our time. In 1949 he released "Riders in the Sky (A Cowboy Legend)," his hit song that is better known as "Ghost Riders in the Sky." It was while working as a seasonal ranger at Death Valley that Stan Jones penned the following lyrics:

> An old cowpoke went riding
> out one dark and windy day,
>
> Up on a ridge he rested as
> he went along his way,
>
> When all at once a mighty herd
> of red-eyed cows he saw,
>
> A ploughin' thru the ragged skies
> and up a cloudy draw.
>
> Yi pi yi ay, Yi pi yi o,
> The ghost herd in the sky.

Born in Douglas, Arizona, in 1914, Stan Jones served in the United States Navy in World War II, obtained a degree in zoology from the University of California, and took a job as a park ranger in Mount Rainier National Park. Far more comfortable in the deserts of the Southwest, he transferred to California's Death Valley National Monument. In 1948, he served as a guide for movie scouts preparing to make the film *3 Godfathers* with John Wayne. One night, Jones performed "Riders in the Sky" for the Hollywood crew while sitting around a campfire. Famed director John Ford eventually heard the handsome ranger sing the ballad and was so impressed he developed a screenplay for a movie of the same name that he made the next year with Gene Autry in a starring role. Ford and Jones formed a lasting friendship.

In discussing the origin of the song, Jones recalled that in his younger days, he and another cowboy, Cap Watts, experienced a summer thunderstorm while working for the D Hill Ranch in southeastern Arizona. The quickly moving clouds suggested phantoms in the sky, and Watts yelled that they were "ghost riders." He proceeded to tell the story of the "ghost riders" who tried to "catch the devil's herd." Jones recalled the yarn years later and set the words to music.

First recorded by Burl Ives, the moving piece has been released by dozens of top singers and musicians. With the success of this mega-hit song, Stan Jones was able to resign from the National Park Service and move with his wife Olive to Hollywood. At Ford's request, Jones wrote the soundtrack for the 1950 Ward Bond film *Wagon Master* and later composed the title song for *The Searchers,* starring John Wayne. During his career in the movie industry, Jones wrote music for both big-screen westerns and Walt Disney television shows; he acted in several of them.

Former park ranger Stan Jones died in Los Angeles on December 13, 1963.

Even underwater, park resources need to be inventoried and protected. This ranger is mapping an archeological site in southern Florida's Biscayne National Park in 1990.
DAN LENIHAN COLLECTION

Using advanced diving skills often needed for emergencies, rangers Mark Forbes (left), Roger Rudolph (center), and Rick Smith (right) practice diving in Yosemite's frozen Merced River in January 1972. AUTHOR'S COLLECTION

On September 24, 1991, a United States cave-diving record was set at 436 feet, in, of all places, Death Valley National Monument.

The Submerged Resources Center has sent divers to work in waters from the tip of the Aleutian Islands to Micronesia, and from France to Hawaii, and it has been involved in 120 projects, many of which have been highlighted in national magazines and television documentaries. The team comprises a core group of eight divers, and these rangers enjoy highly rewarding careers filled with serious adventure.

The center spent many thousands of hours over the course of a decade studying the USS *Arizona*—a sunken ship three times the size of the Statute of Liberty. With over a thousand sailors still entombed and at over six hundred feet in length, it was at the time the biggest man-made object ever mapped by divers. Center divers then later mapped the nine-hundred-foot-long USS *Saratoga* at Bikini Atoll. Nearly two hundred feet below the surface, the *Saratoga* was one of ninety vessels sacrificed when the United States tested an atom bomb in 1946. At the Navy's request, the rangers of the center studied the area and assessed its safety for visitors and returning natives.

Submerged Resources Center divers have been involved in a number of other fascinating projects. Working with French officials, they repeatedly dove to two hundred feet in the English Channel in extremely cold and heavy currents to evaluate the CSS *Alabama*, a Civil War Confederate raider. The group also oversaw the raising of the USS *Hunley*, a Union submarine sunk in 1864, from the depths of Charleston Harbor. Their biggest challenge, however, was the study of sunken ships in northern Lake Superior at Isle Royale National Park that took six seasons. At a depth of 180 feet, the water's pressure and its 34-degree temperature froze regulators and caused lips to go numb in seconds.

A diving bell (center) is readied to search four-hundred-foot-deep Lake Mead for the park's ranger patrol plane in 1970. The three passengers died but the pilot escaped. With the cooperation of the Department of Defense, the submergible was flown in from Florida. DON WEIR PHOTO

RANGERS IN THE AIR

Planes were flying over national parks as early as 1913 (when one made a pass over Glacier), and there is a record of a landing at Yellowstone in 1917. The first aircraft touched down in Yosemite Valley two years later, and park Superintendent W. B. Lewis wrote about the event in his *Annual Report to the Director* and noted that: "the use of the aeroplane for fire patrol . . . should be immediately considered."

As early as 1941, a helicopter was considered for a Park Service rescue; a stunt parachutist needed to be plucked off Wyoming's 865-foot-high Devils Tower. It would be 1949 before one was actually used in a park—Hawaii National Park.

The U.S. Forest Service recognized the value of airplanes as an aid to their work as early as 1920. With the cooperation from the Army Air Corps, "26 planes, 29 officers, 15 cadets, and an average of 92 enlisted men" and "31 national forest officers" were dedicated to aerial fire patrol in the West that summer. Since that first application, aircraft have been routinely used by land management agencies for patrol, rescue, wildlife monitoring, backcountry administration, and a variety of other functions.

Military helicopters such as this Army Chinook with a long line at 13,300 feet on an August 1997 body recovery are critical to successful search and rescue programs in climbing parks such as Mt. Rainier.
MIKE GAUTHIER PHOTO

The National Park Service acquired its first plane in 1936, and has embraced the use of flying machines since. It currently has twenty-six planes, five helicopters, and about thirty pilots in its "Air Force." With the exception of a plane and pilot assigned to a regional office and used mostly for administrative purposes, service planes and their ranger pilots are used at parks having immense tracts of remote lands to manage.

Seventeen of these single-engine planes—most of them equipped with floats—are hangared in Alaska and directly support Denali, Gates of the Arctic, Katmai, Lake Clark, and Wrangell-St. Elias National Parks. The remaining craft are at Big Bend, Cape Hatteras, Death Valley, Glen Canyon (two), Grand Canyon, Lake Mead, and Voyageurs. The United States Park Police operate five helicopters with about a dozen pilots in our nation's capital. The copters are used for patrol, search and rescue, medicals, and policing, as well as for the security of our president as he moves about the region.

Rangers who fly aircraft in the remote, rugged corners of North America engage in some of the most dangerous and demanding aviation in the world. Hunting from the air for illegal mines in the nearly thirteen million acres of Wrangell-St. Elias, a huge assemblage of glaciers and peaks over sixteen thousand feet, is like "looking for a needle in a haystack." Searching for an overdue climber, circling just above the icy slopes of Denali's 20,320-foot-high Mt. McKinley, is tricky at best. Big Bend's pilot routinely flies the Texas-Mexican border, watching for illegal aliens and evidence of drug-related trades, as he soars above the area's broken canyons and mesas.

Ranger-pilots have earned numerous awards for bravery. Voyageur National Park's Scott Evans landed his small plane repeatedly on a remote lake in the middle of a winter snowstorm in 1996 to rescue three seriously injured snowmobilers who were trapped there. His efforts earned him the Department of the Interior Valor Award.

Most ranger-pilots are in "dual function" positions; flying is an important aspect of their jobs, but they have other duties. Just like other field rangers, they are called upon to perform protection, resource management, and other administrative duties within the park, many of them far from any airplane.

The flying program of the National Park Service is overseen by a National Aviation Manager, who makes sure that ranger-pilots follow the guidelines established and monitored by the Department of the Interior's Office of Aircraft Services. During the past several years, pilots from the Interior's nine agencies have flown as many as 100,000 hours annually, including more than 20,000 hours logged by the pilots of the National Park Service.

Not all rangers work in the woods. Gatherings such as this assembly of the "Promise Keepers" on October 4, 1997, occur with some frequency on the National Mall in Washington, D.C. They require a coordinated effort by United States Park Police and park rangers.
TERRY J. ADAMS PHOTO, NATIONAL PARK SERVICE ARCHIVES

"Yellowstone's Children":
Rangers and the World Community

The United States claims proud title to at least two important cultural concepts: democracy and national parks. Our country's national park system has spawned more than thirty thousand protected cultural and natural areas worldwide—dubbed "Yellowstone's Children"—for their genealogical relationship to the world's first designated national park. The international conservation and preservation communities recognize the U.S. National Park Service as a leader in identifying, protecting, and managing key natural and cultural treasures. As both example and mentor, the agency shares its considerable talents, expertise, and experiences in a multitude of global partnerships. This is largely done through the Service's Office of International Affairs.

Every year, for instance, the National Park Service hosts several hundred park and conservation leaders from around the world. They come for formal training, professional conferences, observation and internships, and general orientation with a wide variety of operational programs. Foreign park dignitaries and promising young leaders in politics, economics, and education request briefings and interviews with service personnel. The most successful exchange programs have been in park planning, technical program evaluation, and international training in interpretation, administration, and operations. In 1998 alone, the National Park Service aided forty-one different countries through the efforts of 399 employees, who served from several weeks to many months. As well, seven national parks in five other nations have established "sister park" relationships with areas within the National Park System. Some examples of this cooperative interchange are:

- Restoration advice on the Taj Majal for India;

- Instructing park rangers in SCUBA in Tanzania;

- Obtaining historical documents from archives in Spain;

- Conducting an aboriginal culture study with Australia;

- Management planning for a vital panda reserve in China;

- Planning in the Central Balkans National Park in Bulgaria;

- Park preparation for critical, disappearing habitat in Sri Lanka;

- Advising on eradication efforts of exotic plant species in South Africa;

- Training park staffs in fire fighting and search and rescue in Venezuela; and

- Developing border-shared national parks between the United States and Mexico.

APPENDIX

THE FIFTEEN LARGEST AREAS IN THE NATIONAL PARK SYSTEM

	(ACRES)
State of West Virginia	*15,507,840*
Wrangell-St. Elias National Park & Preserve (AK)	13,176,391
Gates of the Arctic National Park & Preserve (AK)	8,472,512
State of Maryland	*6,694,400*
Noatak National Preserve (AK)	6,569,904
State of Vermont.	*6,152,960*
Denali National Park & Preserve (AK)	6,076,528
State of New Hampshire	*5,938,560*
State of Massachusetts	*5,301,760*
State of New Jersey	*4,983,680*
State of Hawaii	*4,141,440*
Katmai National Park & Preserve (AK)	4,093,240
Lake Clark National Park & Preserve (AK)	4,044,132
Death Valley National Park (CA-NV)	3,367,628
Glacier Bay National Park & Preserve (AK)	3,283,168
State of Connecticut	*3,211,520*
Bering Land Bridge National Preserve (AK)	2,690,179
Yukon-Charley Rivers National Preserve (AK)	2,526,509
Yellowstone National Park (WY-MT-ID)	2,219,791
Kobuk Valley National Park (AK)	1,750,737
Everglades National Park (FL)	1,507,850
Lake Mead National Recreation Area (NV-AZ)	1,495,666
Mojave Desert National Preserve (CA)	1,450,000
State of Delaware	*1,308,160*

There are twenty-one areas within the National Park System larger than the State of Rhode Island (755,680 acres).

At 0.02 acre, Philadelphia's Thaddeus Kosciuszko National Memorial is the smallest area within the System.

THE FIFTEEN BUSIEST AREAS IN THE NATIONAL PARK SYSTEM (RECREATION VISITS IN *2001*)

Blue Ridge Parkway (NC)	19,969,587
Golden Gate National Recreation Area (CA)	13,457,900
Great Smoky Mountains National Park (TN-NC)	9,197,697
Lake Mead National Recreation Area (AZ-NV)	8,465,547
Gateway National Recreation Area (NY)	8,285,059
George Washington Memorial Parkway (MD-VA-DC)	7,664,091
Natchez Trace Parkway (MS-AL-TN)	5,552,351
Delaware Water Gap National Recreation Area (NJ-PA)	4,867,273
Gulf Islands National Seashore (FL-MS)	4,549,900
Cape Cod National Seashore (MA)	4,391,478
Statue of Liberty National Monument (NY)	4,317,998
Chesapeake and Ohio Canal National Historic Park (MD)	4,174,048
Grand Canyon National Park (AZ)	4,104,809
Lincoln Memorial (DC)	3,968,357
Vietnam Veterans Memorial (DC)	3,704,008

There were 279,873,926 recreational visits to the National Park System in 2001. The least visited area was Alaska's Aniakchak National Monument with 206. (*Source:* Tom Wade, National Park Service)

THE FIFTEEN LARGEST BUDGETS IN NATIONAL PARK SERVICE AREAS (PROPOSED BUDGET FOR FISCAL YEAR *2003*)

		(EMPLOYEES[a])
Yellowstone National Park	$27,304,000	556
Yosemite National Park	$23,378,000	562
Gateway National Recreation Area	$20,713,000	359
Grand Canyon National Park	$19,016,000	411
Independence National Historical Park	$18,660,000	208
National Capital Parks—Central	$17,769,000	234
Great Smoky Mountains National Park	$15,483,000	289
Lake Mead National Recreation Area	$14,329,000	230
Everglades National Park	$13,958,000	207
Golden Gate National Recreation Area	$13,958,000	206
Blue Ridge Parkway	$13,442,000	232
Sequoia & Kings Canyon National Parks[b]	$13,161,000	290
Statue of Liberty & Ellis Island	$11,367,000	113

Denali National Park	$11,030,000	89
Shenandoah National Park	$10,584,000	231

For Fiscal Year 2003, the total proposed budget for the National Park Service was $2,731,843,000 and the authorized full-time equivalents (FTEs) were 20,289.

[a] The "Employees" number is based upon FTEs or "Employee Years." This figure reflects the maximum number of people authorized in the budget. One FTE can represent two six-month seasonal positions, four three-month seasonal positions, etc. A "seasonal" park such as Yellowstone may have as many as eight hundred employees working for the government in the summer.

[b] Although established separately and fifty years apart, the two parks are administered jointly.

WHERE RANGERS WORK

National parks are generally large natural areas with exceptional natural, historic, and cultural resources. Hunting, mining, grazing and other resource-consuming activities are not permitted within them, although they may have been at one time. Originally, the president was empowered to create national parks (twenty-one parks came into existence in this way) but now only Congress can authorize a national park.

Under the authority granted in the Antiquities Act of 1906, however, the president may proclaim **"national monuments."** Beginning with Teddy Roosevelt, who created eighteen such areas, thirteen presidents have used this power to establish 126 monuments and related sites (through 2002).

Designations for national **historic sites, memorials, parkways, scenic trails, etc.,** are often made by the body's enabling legislation, but there are no National Park Service guidelines for naming units in the System. Many sites have names that simply describe the resources they protect.

As of the end of 2002, the National Park System included the following different types of areas:

National Battlefield	11
National Battlefield Park	3
National Battlefield Site	1
National Historic Site	78
National Historical Park	40
National Lakeshore	4
National Memorial	28
National Military Park	9
National Monument	73
National Park	57
National Parkway	4

National Preserve	17
National Recreation Area	18
National Reserve	2
National River	6
National Scenic Trail	3
National Seashore	10
National Wild and Scenic River	9
Other	12
TOTAL	385

RANGER MILESTONES

3000 B.C. "Guardian of the Land" concept developed in Mesopotamia.

1300s A.D. English word "ranger" evolved from the Germanic "ring" or "range."

1682 Colonial Virginia assigned "rangers" to protect settlements along rivers.

1696 Caretakers patrolled in a park-like area in Maryland.

1760 Fire warden system inaugurated in Colonial New York.

1791 Park Watchmen authorized, predecessor of the United States Park Police.

1823 Texas Rangers informally organized by Stephen Austin.

1849 Department of Interior established within the Federal Government.

1859 Men on horseback patrolled New York City's Central Park.

1862 First Stetson hat designed, predecessor of ranger "flat hat."

1864 Yosemite Grant Act set aside parts of Yosemite as a state park.

1866 Galen Clark became Guardian of Yosemite and first state park ranger.

1871 John Muir used the term "interpret."

1872 Yellowstone National Park established.

1875 U.S. Deputy Marshall Baronett chased horse thieves across Yellowstone.

1877 First Rules and Regulations promulgated for Yellowstone.

Assistant Superintendent James McCartney instructed to "guard" Yellowstone.

First person died in a national park: James Kenck was shot by Indians in Yellowstone.

1879 James McCawley was the first person arrested in a national park.

1880 Harry Yount hired as Gamekeeper of Yellowstone.

Yount, upon resigning, suggested the need for "seasonal police officers."

1884 Justice of Peace and Constables placed in Yellowstone.

First ranger station built in Yellowstone at Norris Geyser Basin.

1884–85	Yellowstone's Assistant Superintendent Henderson first to be referred to as a "park interpreter."
1886	Army moved into Yellowstone and began protecting the park.
1888	Act of valor in Yellowstone was the first officially recognized in a park.
1890	Yosemite, Sequoia, and General Grant National Parks were established.
1891	Forest Reserve Act eventually led to the creation of National Forests.
	First U.S. Commissioner appointed to Yellowstone.
1894	Yellowstone Protection Act authorized park officials to make arrests.
1898	Eleven men designated "assistant forest agents" in Yosemite and Sequoia.
1900	Yosemite witnessed the first automobile to ever enter a national park.
1902	Sequoia's Deputy Ranger Harry Britten became the first "seasonal ranger."
1905	Park Ranger title officially used for the first time in Sequoia.
	Park Service badge issued to national park rangers.
	Act of February 6 authorized *all* employees in parks to make arrests.
1906	Antiquities Act permitted establishment of national monuments.
1908	Mount Rainier issued first automobile park-entry permit.
1909	Rangers in Sequoia adopted a uniform of military cut.
1911	Glacier National Park bought uniforms for its fifteen rangers.
	Rangers attended the first National Park Conference in Yellowstone.
1914	Wind Cave hired first woman to work in a park ranger-like function.
1915	Yellowstone was the site of the first death in a park from an auto accident.
	National Park Ranger Service was established.
	First "full-fledged" campfire programs in a park began in Mesa Verde.
1916	National Park Service established.
1917	Burnell sisters certified as "nature teachers" in Rocky Mountain.
	First museum established in a park at Mesa Verde.
	Organized winter sports began in western parks.
1918	Yosemite's Claire M. Hodges first woman to perform ranger patrol duties.
1920	Uniform badge saying U.S. PARK RANGER issued nationally.
1922	Ansel Hall appointed as Chief Naturalist of NPS.
1925	Yosemite School of Field Natural History founded.
	Yellowstone hired first permanent female ranger-naturalist.
	Park rangers brought under Civil Service rules.

1926	Sequoia hosted first NPS Chief Ranger's Conference.
1927	First ranger murdered: James Cary shot by bootleggers in Hot Springs.
1928	NPS national office of forest fire suppression established.
1929	Naturalist auto caravans began in Mesa Verde and Yosemite.
	Ranger Charlie Browne received Department of Interior's first Valor Award.
	President Hoover appointed Charlie Browne a permanent National Park Ranger.
	Park naturalists held first national conference.
1930	Junior Nature School established in Yosemite: beginning of Junior Ranger Program.
1931	Colonial National Historical Park hired first two field historians in the NPS.
	NPS began using two-way radios in Mt. Rainier.
1932	Naturalists accompanied airplane tours over Grand Canyon.
1933	NPS Director requested that some field rangers become "wildlife rangers."
1934	Underwater archeology began in North America in Colonial National Historical Park.
	NPS Director officially ended all predator control in parks.
	Dorr Yeager began four-book series on park rangers: *Bob Flame*.
1935	Yellowstone rangers slaughtered hundreds of elk due to overpopulation.
1945	"Green Blood" as a term for highly dedicated park employees probably coined.
1948	Country's first rural Search and Rescue School established in Mount Rainier.
1951	Arrowhead authorized as official symbol of NPS.
	Wildland fire research began in the Everglades.
1952	Twelve men from Sequoia earned first DOI Unit Award for a rescue.
1956	First rangers earned DOI Valor Awards.
1957	"Kowski Kollege," first ranger academy, was established in Yosemite.
	John M. Davis appointed NPS' first servicewide Chief Ranger.
1959	Ranger Jack Morehead became the first NPS employee certified in SCUBA.
1961	President John F. Kennedy established Commission on Status of Women.
1963	Horace M. Albright Training Academy opened at Grand Canyon.

1964   Stephen T. Mather Training Center opened at Harpers Ferry.

1968   Mount Rainier rangers attended Service's first advanced emergency medical training.

1969   Cult-leader Charles Manson captured by rangers in Death Valley.

Still currently used, the NPS Park Ranger badge adopted.

1970   Yosemite's "Riot" launched Service's intense focus on law enforcement.

Consolidated Federal Law Enforcement Training Center (FLETC) authorized.

1971   First servicewide Seasonal Law Enforcement School held at Harpers Ferry.

1974   *Sierra*, the television series highlighting Yosemite rangers, debuted for one season.

Enhanced retirement for park rangers in law enforcement and fire began.

NPS was third wildland fire management agency at the Boise Interagency Fire Center.

1976   Passage of General Authorities Act "streamlined" NPS law enforcement.

1977   Association of National Park Rangers founded with thirty-three members.

1978   First land-management seasonal law enforcement school opened.

1979   Comprised of rangers, Alaska Task Force heightened NPS visibility in state.

1980   George Wright Society founded.

1982   First National Freeman Tilden Award given to Ranger Victor Jackson.

1985   Incident Command System formally adopted by NPS.

1988   National Association for Interpretation formed.

1990   Service established its first two Type II All-Risk Management Teams.

1991   Ranger Museum opened in Yellowstone.

Service's first Type I All-Risk Incident Management Team organized and deployed.

1992   International Ranger Federation formed.

1993   Ranger Nevada Barr began writing NPS and ranger-oriented murder mysteries.

1994   First National Harry Yount Award given to Ranger Joe Fowler.

First Lifetime Harry Yount Award given to Ranger Rick Gale.

Ranger Careers initiated.

1998   National Park Omnibus Management Act—an assessment of law enforcement in parks.

FEDERAL LAWS
IMPACTING RANGERS

National Park rangers use a great many laws, at all levels of government: local, state, and federal. Below is a partial list of significant federal laws that have either affected rangers in the past and/or still guide them today. These titles and simple summaries do not reflect the many wide-ranging aspects, obligations, and/or ramifications the laws may have on either the National Park Service or its employees.

1883   *Act of March 3* Directed the United States Army to protect Yellowstone.

1894   *Yellowstone Protection Act* (16 U.S.C. 24 *et seq.*). Also known as the *Lacey Act*, it authorized making arrests for crimes against wildlife in Yellowstone.

1905   *Act of February 6.* Authorized ALL employees of forest reserves and national parks to make arrests and bring offenders before a United States Commissioner.

1906   *Antiquities Act* (16 U.S.C. 431 *et seq.*). Established the first federal policy protecting and preserving historic and prehistoric sites.

1916   *National Park Service Organic Act* (16 U.S.C. 1 *et seq.*). Created the agency.

1926   *A Civil Service Commission Act* (Executive Order No. 4445). Commission prepared qualifications and examinations for rangers to enter federal government.

1933   *Reorganization Act* (Executive Order Nos. 6166 & 6228). Consolidated existing national parks, monuments, military parks, etc. under the National Park Service.

1935   *Historic Sites, Buildings and Antiquities Act* (16 U.S.C. 461 *et seq.*). Preserves "historic sites, buildings and objects of national significance."

1936   *Park, Parkway, and Recreation Area Study Act* (49 Stat.1894). Resulted in system developing National Seashores, Lakeshores, Recreation Areas, etc.

1936   *Presidential Executive Order* (No. 7332). Authorized ALL Service employees to make arrests and issue citations. Superseded by *General Authorities Act* of 1976.

1948   *Federal Tort Claims Act* (28 U.S.C. 2671 *et seq.*). Waives United States sovereign immunity for compensation of property for negligence by government.

1948   *Arrowhead Law* (18 U.S.C. 701). Protects NPS Arrowhead, badge, and uniform.

1953   *Facilitate the Management of the National Park System* (16 U.S.C. 461
        et seq). Authorizes the agency to render emergency services to
        outside jurisdictions.

1964   *Wilderness Act* (P.L. 88-577). Established the National Wilderness
        Preservation System throughout federal lands, including na-
        tional parks and monuments.

1965   *Concessions Policy Act* (79 Stat. 969). Authorized public accommoda-
        tions and related services within the National Park System.

1965   *Land and Water Conservation Act* (P.L. 88-578). Established a mone-
        tary fund "to assist . . . agencies in meeting present and future
        outdoor recreation demands."

1966   *National Historic Preservation Act* (P.L. 89-665). Amplifies this coun-
        try's responsibility for both public and private antiquity
        programs.

1967   *Clean Air Act* (690 Stat. 322). Enhances air quality protection within
        the System.

1968   *Wild and Scenic Rivers Act* (82 Stat. 906). Establishes a process for
        protecting special rivers and their riparian corridors.

1968   *National Trail Systems Act* (82 Stat. 919). Establishes a process for rec-
        ognizing and enhancing trails having national significance.

1969   *National Environmental Policy Act* (P.L. 91-190). Declared a federal
        policy governing this country's environment.

1970   *General Authorities Act* (P.L. 91-383). Clarified the System's authori-
        ties and amended the Organic Act of 1916 which created the
        National Park Service.

1972   *Clean Water Act* (33 U.S.C. 1251 *et seq.*). Protects the "Nation's
        waters."

1973   *Endangered Species Act* (P.L. 93-205) Protects this country's threat-
        ened and endangered animals and plants.

1974   *Enhanced Retirement Act* (P.L. 93-350). Authorizes a special retire-
        ment for NPS employees engaged in full-time law enforcement
        and/or fire fighting.

1976   *General Authorities Act* (P.L. 91-383). Specifically authorizes rangers
        to make arrests and carry firearms, as well as enhances other
        law enforcement details.

1978   *Redwood National Park Act* (P.L. 90-545). Reasserts the high standard
        of resource protection prescribed by Congress in the Organic
        Act of 1916.

1979   *Archeological Resources Protection Act* (P.L. 96-95). Protects archeological resources on public and Native American lands.

1980   *Alaska National Interest Lands Conservation Act* (P.L. 96-487). Established large tracts of conservation units in Alaska and detailed how they are to be managed.

1990   *Native American Graves Protection and Repatriation Act* (104 Stat. 3048). Protects Native American graves and related funerary and cultural items.

CONTRIBUTORS

Glen Alexander
Shawn Ankrom
Dale Antonich
Bob Barbee
Frank Betts
Bob Binnewies
Bill Blake
Jim Brady
Rhonda Brooks
Paul Broyles
Mark Buktenica
Dennis Burnett
Linda Campbell
Tom Cherry
Steve Clark
Kevin Cochary
Don Coelho
Bruce Collins
Stu Croll
Kevin Daley
Joe Decker
Jon R. Dick
Russ Dickenson
Hugh Dougher
Tom Durant
Linda Eade
Jan Eagle
Mike Ebersole
Darrell Echols
Ward Eldridge
Doug Erskine
Larry Frederick
Steve Frye

Glenn Fulfer
Mary Liz Gale
Rick Gale
Steve Gazzano
John Good
Barbara
  Goodman
Clark Guy
Tom Habecker
Bill Halainen
Elaine Hall
Jim Hannah
John
  Henneberger
Paul Henry
Don Hill
Leigh Hinrichsen
Bob Hoff
Ken Hulick
Hank Johnston
Clayton Jordan
Marsha Karle
Jeff Karraker
Ron Kerbo
Bob Krumenaker
Dan Lenihan
Bruce Lenon
Deb Liggett
Stan Lock
Neil Mangum
Steve Mark
Dick Marks
Bob Marriott

Dick Martin
Jim Martin
Corky Mayo
Steve Medley
Dave Mihalic
Jeri Mihalic
Dave Moore
Doug Morris
Julie Mossman
Rick Mossman
Dave Nathanson
Ed Nelson
Pete Nigh
Deb Noreen
Rick Obernesser
Jeff Ohlfs
Bill Orr
Cindy Ott-Jones
Dave Panebaker
Dave Patterson
Jerry Pendleton
Jack Potter
John Quinley
Bob Reid
J.T. Reynolds
Gene Rose
Ginny Rousseau
Roger Rudolph
Shirley Sargent
Dick Sellars
Todd Seuss
Elaine Sevy
Lee Shackleton

Steve Shackleton
Deirdre Shaw
Rick Smith
Bill Sontag
Bill Spruill
Chris Stein
Darrell Stone
Jeff Sullivan
Ron Sutton
Steve Swanke
Bill Tanner
Jim Tilmant
John Townsend
Lisa Towery
Tom Tschol
Gail Van Slyke
Larry Van Slyke
Bill Wade
Tom Wade
Mike Warren
Mike Watson
Vicki Webster
Lee Whittlesey
Sheila Williams
Rosa Wilson
Jennifer Wolk
Bryce Workman
Chuck Young

FOR FURTHER READING

Most park visitor centers and bookstores will have material both specific to that particular area as well as ones that are more generalized about the National Park System.

Albright, Horace M. *Oh, Ranger!* Stanford, CA: Stanford University Press, 1928.

———. *Creating the National Park Service: The Missing Years*. Norman: University of Oklahoma Press, 1999.

———. *The Birth of the National Park Service: The Founding Years*. Salt Lake City, UT: Howe Brothers, 1985.

Barr, Nevada. *Track of the Cat*. New York: G. P. Putnam's Sons, 1993.

———. *A Superior Death*. New York: G. P. Putnam's Sons, 1994.

———. *Ill Wind*. New York: G. P. Putnam's Sons, 1995.

Berkowitz, Paul D. *U.S. Rangers: The Law of the Land*. Redding, CA: CT Publishing Co., 1995.

Everhart, William C. *The National Park Service*. Boulder, CO: Westview, 1983.

———. *Take Down Flag & Feed the Horses*. Chicago: University of Illinois Press, 1998.

Farabee, Charles R. *Death, Daring and Disaster: Search and Rescue in the National Parks*. Boulder, CO: Roberts Rinehart, 1998.

Garrison, Lemuel A. *The Making of a Ranger*. Salt Lake City, UT: Howe Brothers, 1983.

Gildhart, Robert C. (Bert). *Montana's Early-Day Rangers*. Helena, MT: Montana Magazine, 1985.

Hampton, H. Duane. *How the U.S. Cavalry Saved Our National Parks*. Bloomington, IN: University Press, 1971.

Hartzog, George B., Jr. *Battling for the National Parks*. Mt. Kisco, NY: Moyer Bell Limited, 1988

Henneberger, John W. *Chronology of the Ranger Story*. Corvallis, OR: Author, 3256 NW Harrison Blvd., 1996.

Johnston, Hank. *The Yosemite Grant: 1864–1906 A Pictorial History*. Yosemite, CA: The Yosemite Association, 1995.

Kaufman, Polly Welts. *National Parks and the Woman's Voice: A History*. Albuquerque: University of New Mexico Press, 1996.

Lenihan, Daniel. *Submerged: Adventures of America's Most Elite Underwater Archeology Team.* New York: Newmarket, 2002.

Lynch, Michael G. *Rangers of California's State Parks: 125 Years of Park Protection and Service.* Auburn, CA: Author, Post Office Box 3212, 1996.

Mackintosh, Barry. *The National Parks: Shaping the System.* Division of Publications and the Employee Development Division. National Park Service. Washington, DC: GPO, 1991.

Moomaw, Jack C. *Recollections of a Rocky Mountain Ranger.* Estes Park, CO: YMCA of the Rockies, 1994.

Murphy, Bob. *Desert Shadows.* Morongo Valley, CA: Sagebrush Press, 1993.

Pyne, Stephen J. *Fire on the Rim.* New York: Weidenfeld & Nicholson, 1989.

Rettie, Dwight F. *Our National Park System: Caring for America's Greatest Natural and Historic Treasures.* Chicago: University of Illinois Press, 1995

Sargent, Shirley. *Protecting Paradise: Yosemite Rangers, 1898–1960.* Yosemite, CA: Ponderosa, 1998.

Sellars, Richard West. *Preserving Nature in the National Parks: A History.* New Haven, CT: Yale University Press, 1998.

Sholly, Dan R. *Guardians of Yellowstone.* New York: Morrow, 1991.

Wellman, Mark and John Finn. *Climbing Back.* Waco, TX: WRS Publishers, 1992.

Wirth, Conrad L. *Parks, Politics, and the People.* Norman: University of Oklahoma Press, 1980.

INDEX

Page numbers followed by *b*, *i*, or *p* refer to boxed text, illustrations, or photographs respectively.

KEN HULICK PHOTO